SHOPPING GUIDE TO
JAPAN

What to buy, where to buy it, and how to get the most for your ¥en!

BOYÉ LAFAYETTE DE MENTE

TUTTLE PUBLISHING
Tokyo • Rutland, Vermont • Singapore

Other Books by the Author

"Japan is the shopping capital of the world—
unequalled in the number, variety and convenience of
its shops, malls and street arcades!"

—the author

First published in 2007 by Tuttle Publishing, an imprint of Periplus Editions (HK) Ltd., with editorial offices at 364 Innovation Drive, North Clarendon, Vermont 05759.

ISBN-13: 978-4-8053-0876-9
ISBN-10: 4-8053-0876-1

Distributed by:

North America
Tuttle Publishing
364 Innovation Drive
North Clarendon, VT 05759-9436
Tel: 1 (802) 773-8930; Fax: 1 (802) 773-6993
Email: info@tuttlepublishing.com
Website: www.tuttlepublishing.com

Japan
Tuttle Publishing
Yaekari Building, 3rd Floor
5-4-12 Osaki, Shinagawa-ku, Tokyo
Japan 141-0032
Tel: (81) 03 5437-0171; Fax: (81) 03 5437-0755
Email: tuttle-sales@gol.com

Asia Pacific
Berkeley Books Pte Ltd
130 Joo Seng Road #06-01
Singapore 368357
Tel: (65) 6280-1330; Fax: (65) 6280-6290
Email: inquiries@periplus.com.sg
Website: www.periplus.com

11 10 09 08 07   5 4 3 2 1

Printed in Singapore

Contents

A Shopper's Shangri La

Since the early 1960s Japan has been one of the shopping Meccas of the world—for visitors as well as residents.

The Japanese are among the world's most dedicated and demanding shoppers, and given the level of affluence and the concentration of over 126 million people in just a few population centers, it is not surprising that the shopping scene in Japan is itself a sight to see.

The Japanese love-affair with shopping began in the mid–1950s and came of age in the 1980s, by which time a wide variety of electric and electronic devices had been added to the traditional arts and crafts that had attracted foreign visitors as far back as the 16th century.

The number and variety of retail outlets in Japan, their size and sophistication, can be overwhelming to many visitors. Despite the density of stores, shops, and shoppers, however, there is structure and order in the Japanese marketplace— making it an adventure rather than a chore.

Many urban neighborhoods, which often retain their village origins, have their own **shotengai** (*show-tane-guy*) or shopping street, where one normally finds a meat shop, fish vendor, produce shop, house wares stores, stationery shop, drugstore, electrical appliance store, beauty parlor, barber shop, dry cleaner, a few small restaurants, a bar or two, and so on.

Shopping in neighborhood shotengai, which are generally

within walking distance for most residents in the neighborhood, is therefore much less of a hassle than shopping in the major centers. The shoppers have often known the shopkeepers since childhood, making the experience a community affair.

Virtually all of the busy commuter railway stations in Japan's larger cities are hubs of shopping activity. The largest ones are virtual cities within themselves, with major department stores and every other conceivable type of store, plus dozens to hundreds of restaurants, coffee shops and bars that attracts hundreds of thousands of people on a daily basis.

Most of Japan's large shopping districts began as neighborhood shopping streets and expanded as the population grew, resulting in the construction of interconnected transportation systems.

The famous Ginza district in central Tokyo is probably the country's best-known shopping area, and within a distance of some four blocks of the center of the Ginza district there are six interconnected subway lines and a train station that serves major commuter lines.

In addition to the Ginza district there are more than a hundred other shopping districts in Tokyo, including Shibuya, Shinjuku, Ueno, Nihonbashi and Ikebukuro—which are as large as many cities.

The main branch of the Mitsukoshi Department Store, the oldest department store in the world, is in the Nihonbashi business and shopping district—which was the center of Tokyo until it was overshadowed by the Ginza in the late 1800s.

The predecessor of today's famous Mitsukoshi, Ltd. was the Echigoya dry goods store, founded in Nihonbashi in the late seventeenth century. As Japan became more westernized at the end of the nineteenth century, Echigoya began to handle products other than dry goods, and in the process became the first real department store in Japan—and in the world.

Since then, Japanese department stores have undergone numerous changes, and today's stores are among the finest in the world. The size of the larger stores, the variety of merchandise they carry, the sophistication of their displays, and the range of social and cultural services they provide is truly amazing.

Altogether there are approximately 1.6 million retail stores in Japan, including 230,000 that sell apparel and accessories, 172,000 that sell furniture and household goods, and 70,000 that sell ladies' and children's clothing. The country boasts over 78,000 bookstores (compared to less than half that number in the United States).

The aim of this book is to provide general guidelines for shopping in this amazing marketplace, including descriptions of the different types of shops and stores, advice on how and where to shop, conversion tables of Japanese sizes and the metric system, essential shopping vocabulary and phrases, and other information important for shopping in Japan.

Whether your interest is in folk craft items that have been made the same way for hundreds of years, or the newest creation by one of Japan's trendy designers, you are sure to find many things that will make the experience worthwhile.

Japan's unique handicrafts make up one of the most important categories of items that both domestic and foreign travelers in Japan buy. And like virtually everything else in Japan, the Japanese handicraft industry is not only officially recognized, it is also defined and structured.

The Ministry of Economy, Trade & Industry has designated precisely 206 crafts as authentic Japanese handicrafts—under a law that refers to them as **Dento-teki Kogeihin** (*Dane-toh-tay-kee Koh-gay-e-heen*), or "Traditional Handicrafts".

The law says that an item must meet the following requirements to qualify as a handicraft:

1) It must be used mainly in daily life, such as in funerals, weddings, festivals, etc.

2) It must be hand-made, and must reflect the beauty that has long been associated with Japanese arts and crafts—a beauty referred to as **yo-no-bi** (*yoh-no-be*).

3) It must be made using traditional techniques and technology—but modern machinery may be used if the finished item maintains all of its traditional characteristics.

4) It must have been made continuously for 100 or more years.

5) There must be a minimum of ten craft shops and 30 craftsmen in a specific area making a particular item before it can be recognized as a traditional handicraft.

Not surprisingly, the area in Japan that has the largest number of officially recognized handicrafts is the former Imperial capital of Kyoto, which has 17. Niigata Prefecture is next with 14, Aichi Prefecture follows with 12, Tokyo has 11 and Ishikawa Prefecture has ten.

These areas, and all of the other prefectures, promote their designated handicrafts through advertising and permanent exhibits at key locations.

There are also many unusual items in Japan that foreigner shoppers should be aware of: bedding and wearing apparel made of materials that have anti-bacterial and odor-suppressing qualities; pillows that adjust to the level of humidity in the air, and sonic toothbrushes that vibrate 31,000 times per minute and remove 36 percent of the plaque buildup, etc.

To find these and other advanced high-tech items in Japan go to the nearest Tokyu Hands store.

Methods of Payment

Until the last decades of the 20th century most Japanese shoppers paid cash for their purchases, whether they were for short-term or long-term needs, particularly in smaller shops and stores.

Since then the use of credit cards and debit cards has become routine in department stores, other major retail outlets and in a continuously growing number of upscale shops, restaurants and the like. With the exception of small restaurants, bars and clubs, most businesses that cater to foreign visitors accept credit cards.

The latest evolution in the payment process is the use of electronic cash stored in smart cards and mobile phones. Over 26 million Japanese now use smart cards and phones for small payments, including subway and train fares, restaurant bills, store purchases and vending machines. The use of electronic cash is rapidly becoming the norm.

Hotels and a few department stores provide currency exchange services for those who need cash to pay for incidentals such as bus, subway and train fares, and for bills at typical restaurants and other shops. There are also ATMS at banks in the vicinity of most transportation stations.

Personal checks and money orders are rarely used in Japan, and generally are not accepted by most businesses.

Most Japanese who use public transportation regularly buy weekly or monthly passes. Daily and weekly transpiration passes are also available for foreign visitors—which not only eliminates the need for cash to buy tickets, it also eliminates the need for checking the fare (on large fare boards above the ticket machines) each time you board a subway or train.

Public transportation passes can be purchased at the airports where visitors enter Japan, as well as from offices located in primary subway and train stations.

"Point Cards"

As in the United States and other countries, large numbers of Japanese stores have what is called "point cards," meaning that every time you buy something you get "points," and after you get enough of them you can exchange them for free products or discounts. Some stores will give you a "point card" for the asking. Others want you to fill out an application form.

Prices in Japan

Consumer prices in Japan have come down on many items since the go-go days of the 1960s, 70s and 80s, when imports were strictly controlled and many products, both imported and domestic, were priced at three to five times what they cost abroad.

Prices were kept artificially high in order to generate extraordinary profits that were used to build up more export capability and to make investments abroad.

Freeing of the market for the importation of foreign goods in the 1970s and 80s, combined with the virtual collapse of Japan's financial system in 1990–1, has forced dramatic reductions in many prices, from clothing and food items to medicines.

As in other countries, prices of the same or similar items can vary dramatically in Japan, depending on the image and reputation of the retailer. Upscale shops in upscale locations set their prices accordingly.

It therefore pays to take advantage of the well-known bargain and discount retailers and bargain shopping centers in each city. Tokyo's Akihabara district is world-famous for its low prices on appliances, computers, other electronic devices, musical instruments, and software.

Consumption Taxes

Japan's retail trade is obliged to collect 5 percent in consumption taxes on all goods sold, but the taxes are included in the listed prices so in most cases it is not an obvious charge. A few places list both pre-tax and taxed prices on their goods. See more on consumption taxes below.

Tax-Free Goods

One of the steps the Japanese government took back in the early 1950s to encourage tourism was to make it possible for shops with the necessary license to sell goods to people who are in the country on tourist visas.

These tax-free shops are concentrated in the major cities where visitors do most of their shopping. It should be noted, however, that the categories of merchandise that can be sold tax-free to tourists is prescribed by the government.

All items in shops that promote themselves as tax-free shops (in their advertisements and on their storefronts) are not necessarily tax-free. The items themselves may or may not have tags on them that say "tax-free", depending on the store policy. If they do not have tags, ask a clerk if they are tax-free.

Store Hours

Most retail shops and stores in Japan open at 10 a.m., and stay open until 7 or 8 p.m., although this varies in some locations and with some types of stores.

Three of the largest convenience market chains—Family Mart, Seven-Eleven and Lawson's—are open 24 hours a day, seven days a week. This has led a number of supermarkets to go on 24–7 schedules, and the number appears to be growing. Many stores extend their hours on special days, such as festivals.

Most of Japan's large retail outlets as well as many personal service shops are open on Sundays, and Sundays are the biggest shopping day in the country. Some of these shops are closed on Mondays; others close on Wednesdays or Thursdays.

Discount Days

All department stores and most other retail shops in Japan stage "discount days" during the year, with two of the longest periods being the June and July mid-summer gift-giving period (**O'chugen**/*Oh-chuu-gane*), and the December end-of-the-year gift-giving season (**O'seibo**/*Oh-say-ee-boe*). This event also spills over into January.

In some stores, discounts can be up to 70 percent off the regular retail price, so if you are in Japan during these seasons, it pays to take advantage of these events.

In some places and for some events (as is the case in other countries), these bargain sales bring out the primitive in people, including grandmothers who can behave like linebackers in a football game.

Store Etiquette

Traditionally in Japan store clerks did not approach customers and offer to help them. Such behavior was regarded as rude. They waited for the shopper to indicate that he or she wanted service.

Those stationed near entrances would, however, called out **irasshaimase**! (*ee-rah-shy-mah-say*)—Welcome! to everyone who entered the store.

This custom still prevails in many upscale stores especially among main store employees. But it has become common for employees of independent vendors in department stores and such to take the initiative when customers come near them.

It is also common in independent shops that cater to visitors for clerks to approach customers and offer their help.

There is, however, an ongoing tradition of salespeople tending sidewalk displays and those working in the food departments of major department stores to call out loudly and continuously to all passersby, shouting a variety of things to get their attention.

Other shops that are traditional in design and in the merchandise they carry have also carried on the tradition of employers calling out to potential customers. This is especially common in market places where there are dozens of shops competing for business.

This custom makes for a rousing atmosphere on shopping streets and in shopping areas throughout Japan.

The behavior of clerks and other employees in most Japanese stores remains subdued and formal. In department stores, especially, clerks do not chat with each other, read or do anything that would detract from them being alert to the presence of customers.

One of the things that is most impressive about Japanese department stores in particularly is that in most of them when the stores open at 10 a.m. each morning all of the floor managers line up at the main entrances to personally and formally welcome customers.

In the case of many traditionally styled bars, cabarets and restaurants it is customary to greet customers loudly, and bid them farewell with the same gusto.

Returns & Refunds

There is a law in Japan that says retail stores must accept faulty products if they are returned within eight days—and stores generally honor this obligation without fuss because just carrying much less selling a defective product results in the loss of face and store image.

However, most stores are less enthusiastic about taking back products that are returned simply because the buyer changed his or her mind. If products have been unwrapped and/or de-boxed, many stores will not accept them.

If you are buying something that you are not positive you will keep, it is best to check the store's returns policy before you buy. There is less, and sometimes no resistance, if you ask for an exchange rather than a refund.

Japanese shoppers are very careful about what they buy, and are generally not caught up in this kind of situation—

unless there is a hidden defect in the product that does not come to light until they try to use it.

Bargaining

It is not customary for department stores and other high-end stores in Japan to engage in bargaining. This said, I myself have asked for a discount in a name department store and got it—which is something normal Japanese would not do.

The Japanese are well aware that bargaining is traditional in many countries, and are not surprised or shocked when a foreigner asks for a discount. Tourists-oriented shops in particular will generally give a discount if asked, especially if one is making a fairly large purchase. They all appear to have a built-in cushion in their prices to accommodate customers.

Bargaining is customary, however, in flea markets and at such places as sidewalk carts and stalls at festivals and other public events.

¥100, ¥300 & ¥1000 Stores

The slow-down in Japan's economy in the early 1990s resulted in the appearance of so-called ¥100 stores in larger cities throughout the country.

One of the reasons for the popularity of the stores is that many consumers treat them more or less like they do at flea markets, and go looking for bargains. Among the items to be found in these shops: clothing, accessories, knick-knacks, kitchen utensils, gardening tools and food.

Others have jumped on the set-price bandwagon, and there are now ¥300 and ¥1000 stores that handle a larger variety and higher quality merchandise.

These set-price stores add the appropriate taxes to your purchase, so you pay ¥105 for a ¥100 item.

CHAPTER 1

Using Japan's
Amazing Subway Systems

Japan has one of the most comprehensive and efficient public transportation systems in the world, made up of city and rural area bus service, commuter train lines within cities and their satellite areas, subway lines and long-distance trains that span the chain of islands.

This vast combination of transportation services is especially convenient and practical because all of the different types are integrated into a network that makes it possible for passengers to transfer to the different services at thousands of hub stations.

The subway lines in Japan's major cities are especially practical for tourists because they provide service to all of the main dining and shopping centers.

Subway Lines in Tokyo

All of the larger and more popular areas of Tokyo are served by two or more subway lines—in some cases with as many as five stations in different parts of the individual districts.

There are 13 subway lines in Tokyo operated by two different companies—one private and the other owned by the city.

Although the lines interconnect at many stations, they are managed separately, sometimes resulting in special tickets and the use of special turnstiles being necessary when transferring from the lines of one company to the lines of the other operator. [This potential problem can be totally avoided by buying and using 1-day or 1-week passes that are good on all of the lines.]

All of the lines are color-coded, and the stations are numbered in sequence from the beginning to the end of each line. Most station lobbies have large wall-maps above or adjoining the ticket vending machines, showing all of the stops and the cost from that particular station.

Several other railways in the capital, notably the Tokyo Waterfront Railway, also qualify as metro (subway) by most definitions.

Tokyo's subway lines have stations that connect with commuter train lines, including JR (Japan Railways) and private lines such as the Keio, Odakyu, and Tobu lines.

In Tokyo the famous Ginza shopping district is served by the Ginza, Marunouchi, Hibiya, Chiyoda, Mita, Yurakucho, and Toei Asakusa lines. The electronic mecca of Akihabara is served by the Ginza, Hibiya and Toei Shinjuku Lines. The popular Omotesando district is served by the Ginza, Hanzomon and Chiyoda Lines, with stations at the east and west ends of the tree-shop-and-restaurant lined boulevard.

Virtually every one of the Tokyo's main **shotengai** (*show-tane-guy*) or "shopping streets" in both business and residential districts throughout the city has one or more subway stations. Several of Tokyo's leading department stores, including Mitsukoshi, Matsuya, Takashimaya, and Isetan are connected to subway stations via basement concourses (so you don't have to get out in bad weather).

All subway stations are designated by street entrances [with many entrances also in large office buildings and department stores]. Stations have large wall signs that depict the various lines, intersecting stations and the cost (fare) to each station. If you cannot find the fare to your destination, just buy the cheapest ticket and pay the balance when you arrive—either to the exit attendant or to a special vending machine available for that purpose.

Banks of ticket vending machines are either below or near the network wall maps. The two subway companies in Tokyo generally accept each other's tickets. If you encounter a situation where they do not, ask the attendant at the window adjoining the entry/exit turnstiles.

As noted above, the best approach for visitors is to buy a day-long or week-long pass at one of the main stations that is good on all of the lines, so that you do not have to worry about fares and transfers.

I recommend that you order a copy of my book Subway Guide to Tokyo prior to your arrival in Japan—or pick one up after you arrive. It covers all of the 13 subway lines in the city, all of the stations and precise station exits for over 500 of the most popular destinations in the city, including all of the shopping areas. [If not available in your local store, the book can be ordered from Amazon.com.]

The subway guide includes detailed information on buying tickets and passes, on transferring lines, and on locating the most convenient exits. Most of the destinations in Tokyo that you may want or need to go to are listed in the book, with the line to take, the station where you should disembark, and the exit you should use.

Subway Lines in Yokohama

Yokohama has four subway lines. One line runs from **Kannai** (*kahn-nie*) through **Kamiooka** (*kah-me-ooh-kah*) on the southwest side to **Shonandai** (*shoh-nahn-die*). Another line runs from Kannai through Yokohama and Shin-Yokohama to **Azamino** (*ah-zah-me-no*).

The **Minato Mirai** (*me-nah-toh me-rie*) Line runs from

Yokohama Central Station along the new habor-side development area. This subway is operated jointly with the Tokyu Toyoko commuter railway, which runs from Yokohama to Shibuya in Tokyo (35 min).

The Minato Mirai Line has both express and local trains, with all trains stopping at Minato Mirai and the terminus station Motomachi-Chukagai.

The Kanazawa Seaside Line is a 10 km elevated fully automated light rail line running south from Shin-Sugita JR Railway Station to Kanazawa-Hakkei station on the Keikyu Railway. The fourth line runs from Hiyoshi to Nakayama.

These lines have stations in all of the main shopping areas of Yokohama.

Subway Lines in Nagoya

Nagoya has six subway lines. Color-coded and thoroughly bilingual, they are easy to navigate and provide easy access to the city's primary shopping districts and attractions.

Subway Lines in Kyoto

Kyoto has two subway lines: the inner city south-north **Karasuma** (*kah-rah-suu-mah*) Line and the east-west **Tozai** (*Toh-zie*) Line. The two lines intersect at Karasuma Oike. Kyoto's subways are decorated with colorful **fusuma** (*fuu-suu-mah*) wall panel scenes taken from Nijo Castle, the residence of the Shoguns when they visited the Imperial city during the Tokugawa era (1603-1868).

Subway Lines in Osaka

All of Osaka's primary shopping districts are served by subways. The city's subway system also plays an important role
in connecting the city center of Osaka to many of its satellite
cities. The Osaka Municipal Transportation Bureau operates 7
subway lines and 1 New Tram line, providing the fastest and
easiest way to get around Osaka.

Each subway line is color-coded for easy identification. All
subway lines operate from 5:00a.m. to around midnight.

There are three subway stations in the downtown district of
Umeda. Umeda station on the Midosuji Line, Higashi-Umeda
station on the Tanimachi Line and Nishi-Umeda station on the
Yotsubashi Line.

You can exit one of these stations and transfer to two other
available subway lines. The method of transfer varies according to the type of ticket you have. Ask the station attendant
which ticket you should buy if you intend to transfer from one
line to another.

Subway Lines in Kobe

There are two subway lines in Kobe: the Seishin-Yamate Line
and the Kaigan Line.

Kobe's first subway, the 22.7 km, 16 station Seishin-Yamate
or Kobe Municipal Subway line, opened in 1977. It is run by
the Hokushin-Kyuko Railway. Kobe's second subway is the 7.9
km Kaigan ("Coast") Line. It opened in July, 2001. Each terminus intersects with the Seishin-Yamate subway, and is mostly
(6.6 km) underground.

Kobe has five separate mass transit facilities: the Kobe
Rapid Railways, the Seinshin Subway, the Hanshin underground, the Portliner elevated guideway, and the Rokko-Liner
light metro.

Subway Lines in Sendai

Sendai has a single north-south (Izumi Chuo Station - Tomizawa Station) subway line. The Tozai (East-West) Line will be opened in 2015, making the Kawauchi and Aobayama campuses of Tohoku University easily accessible from Sendai Station and the city center.

Subway Lines in Sapporo

There are three subway lines in Sapporo: Nanboku-line (green), Tozai-line (red) and Toho-line (blue). They connect with all of the key areas of the city.

CHAPTER 2

A Note on Pronouncing Japanese

The Japanese language is one of the world's easiest languages to pronounce. It consists of a precise number of syllables that are based on only six key sounds.

Five of the six key sounds of Japanese are represented by the English vowel letters a, i, u, e and o. The five vowels in this list are pronounced as follows:

A (*ah*)

I (*ee*)

U (*uu*)

E (*eh*)

O (*oh*)

The sixth key sound in the Japanese language is re-presented in English as the "n" sound, and in Japanese is pronounced like the "n" in bond. For example, **pan**, the Japanese word for bread, is pronounced *pahn*.

These vowels and the n sound are "syllables" in themselves, and the vowels are combined with consonants to produce all the other syllables in the Japanese language.

For example, the five vowel sounds plus the consonant k combine to produce **ka**, **ki**, **ku**, **ke** and **ko**, and are pronounced "*kah, kee, kuu, kay,*" and "*koh.*"

Combining "**s**" with the five vowels results in the syllables **sa**, **shi**, **su**, **se** and **so,** pronounced *sah, she, suu, say, so.* Combining "**t**" with the vowels gives you **ta**, **chi**, **tsu**, **te**, **to** (*tah, chee, 't'sue, tay, toe*).

Next comes **na**, **ni**, **nu**, **ne**, **no** (*nah, nee, nuu, nay, no*), making the order and pronunciation of words in the vowel-based language obvious.

Most syllables in Japanese are distinctly pronounced. At times, however, the **i** and **u** sounds are weak and not sounded out. For example in the word **desu** (which is the verb "to be"), the "**u**" remains silent, and the word is pronounced as "*dess.*"

Another example: in Asakusa (a famous district in Tokyo), the "**u**" is silent and the word is pronounced as *ah-sahk-sah*)— or *ah-sock-sah*, to make it even clearer.

So how would you pronounce **Akasaka Mitsuke** (a famous intersection in Tokyo? (The answer: *Ah-kah-sah-kah Meet-sue-kay*). And how about Tokyo's most famous electronic and electric product shopping district, **Akihabara**? The answer: *Ah-kee-hah-bah-rah*.

CHAPTER 3

Shopping Language

To fully enjoy the shopping experience in Japan it helps if you know a number of key Japanese words and expressions. This does not mean that you must have an extensive shopping vocabulary because sales clerks and others in shops catering to visitors usually know the English terms for the things they sell and understand other shopping terms.

It is helpful and satisfying, however, to know a few basic Japanese greetings and set expressions used by store personnel.

Expressions You May Hear

Following are some basic expressions you are likely to hear while shopping:

Irasshaimase! (*Ee-rah-shy-mah-say!*) Welcome!

Nani wo sashiagemasho ka?
(*Nah-nee oh sah-she-ah-gay-mah-show kah?*)
May I help you?

Sho-sho omachi kudasai.
(*Show-show oh-mah-chee kuu-dah-sie.*)
Just a moment, please.

Omachido sama deshita
(*Oh-mah-chee-doh sah-mah desh-tah*)
I'm sorry I kept you waiting.

Kore wa ikaga desu ka?
(*Koe-ray wah ee-kah-gah dess kah?*) How about this?

Uchi ni wa gozaimasen.
(*Uu-chee nee wah go-zie-mah-sen.*)
We don't have (carry) it.

Uri-kirete orimasu.
(*Uu-ree-kee-ray-tay oh-ree-mahss.*) It's sold out.

Domo arigato gozaimashita
(*Doh-moe ah-ree-gah-toe go-zie-mahssh-tah*)
Thank you very much.

Mata otachiyori kudasai.
(*Mah-tah oh-tah-chee-yoe-ree kuu-dah-sie.*)
Please come again.

Omachi shite imasu. (*Oh-mah-chee sshtay ee-mahss.*)
We'll be waiting for you.

Expressions You Can Use

Following are some basic expressions that you should use
when the occasion arises because it is a courteous and "feel
good" thing to do.

Good morning (said until about 11 a.m.).
Ohayo gozaimasu. (*Oh-hah-yoe go-zie-mahss*)

Good morning/Good day
(said from about 11 a.m. until the early evening).
Konnichi wa. (*Kone-nee-chee wah*)

Good evening
(said from around dusk until the late hours).
Komban wa. (*Kome-bahn wah*)

Note: In the late afternoon and early evening, when neither **kon-nichi wa** nor **komban wa** seems right, it is common for people to use an expression like **domo** (*doe-moe*), which is simply a polite way of recognizing a person's presence. It is usually accompanied by a slight nod.

Good night! **Oyasumi nasai!** (*Oh-yah-suu-me nah-sie*)

I'm looking for _____.
_____ **wo sagashite imasu.**
_____ (*oh sah-gah-ssh-tay ee-mahss.*)

Do you have _____?
_____ **ga arimasu ka,**
(_____ *gah ah-ree-mahss kah?*)

I'd like to buy _____.
_____ **wo kaitai desu.**
(_____ *oh kie-tie dess.*)

Excuse me. Where are the _____?
Sumimasen. _____ **wa doko desu ka?**
(*Sue-me-mah-sen.* _____ *wah doe-koe dess kah?*)

What floor is it on?
Nan kai desu ka? (*Nahn kie dess kah?*)

Please let me see that one. **Are wo misete kudasai.**
(*Ah-ray oh me-say-tay kuu-dah-sie.*)

How much is this? **Kore wa ikura desu ka?**
(*Koe-ray wah ee-kuu-rah dess kah?*)

How much is that? **Sore wa ikura desu ka?**
(*Soe-ray wah ee-kuu-rah dess kah?*)

Do you have a larger one?
Motto okii no ga arimasu ka?
(*Mote-toe oh-kee no gah ah-ree-mahss kah?*)

Do you have a smaller one?
Motto chiisai no ga arimasu ka?
(*Mote-toe chee-sie no gah ah-ree-mahss kah?*)

May I try it on? **Kite mite mo ii desu ka?**
(*Kee-tay mee-tay moe ee dess kah?*)

I'll take this. **Kore wo itadakimasu.**
(*Koe-ray oh ee-tah-dah-kee-mahss*)

I'll take that. **Sore wo itadakimasu.**
(*Soe-ray oh ee-tah-dah-kee-mahss*)

Do you have wrapping paper?
Tsutsumi-gami ga arimasu ka?
(*T'sue-t'sue-me-gah-me gah ah-ree-mahss kah?*)

Please wrap it up. **Tsutsunde kudasai.**
(*T'sue-t'soon-day kuu-dah-sie*)

Please put it in a box. **Hako ni irete kudasai.**
(*Hah-koe nee ee-ray-tay kuu-dah-sie*)

Do you deliver? **Haitatsu ga dekimasu ka?**
(*Hie-tot-sue gah deh-key-mahss kah?*)

Please deliver it to my hotel.
Hoteru e todokete kudasai.
(*Hoe-tay-rue eh toe-doe-kay-tay kuu-dah-sie*)

Please deliver it to my home.
Uchi e todokete kudasai.
(*Uu-chee eh toe-doe-kay-tay kuu-dah-sie*)

Counting in Japanese

In Japan there are two sets of cardinal numbers for counting from one through ten—one set is native Japanese and the other set was imported from China nearly two thousand years ago. The Japanese set is generally used only for counting certain things from one through ten. The Chinese set is used for counting certain things from one through ten as well as all numbers above ten.

Some facility with numbers is, of course, an important part of successful shopping anywhere. While the Japanese numeric system appears complicated at first glance, it is not really very difficult...and if you mistakenly use a Chinese number when a Japanese number is the common one, you will still be understood.

The Japanese Set of Numbers

1 **hitotsu** (*he-toe-t'sue*)
2 **futatsu** (*fuu-tah-t'sue*)
3 **mittsu** (*meet-sue*)
4 **yottsu** (*yoat-sue*)
5 **itsutsu** (*ee-t'sue-t'sue*)
6 **muttsu** (*moot-sue*)
7 **nanatsu** (*nah-naht-sue*); also: **nana** (*nah-nah*)
8 **yattsu** (*yaht-sue*)
9 **kokonotsu** (*koe-koe-no-t'sue*)
10 **to** (*toe*)

The Chinese Set of Numbers

ichi (*ee-chee*)
ni (*nee*)
san (*sahn*)
shi (*she*); **yo** (yoe); **yon** (*yoan*)
go (*go*)
roku (*roe-kuu*)
shichi (*she-chee*)

hachi (*hah-chee*)
kyu (*cue*), **ku** (*kuu*);
ju (*juu*)

The Japanese set of numbers is generally used in units of one through ten when the object or thing concerned is not in a category by itself. For example, if you want two orders of French fries you say:

Furenchi furai futatsu kudasai.
(*Fuu-ren-chee fry fuu-tot-sue kuu-dah-sie*).

In a pinch, you can use the Japanese set of numbers for counting almost anything. However, Japanese has special sets of numeratives for counting certain things, especially items with particular shapes or specific functions, and these numeratives are combined with the Chinese set of numbers when counting such things.

For example, flat things like paper, trays, or plates take the numerative **mai** (*my*). To ask for two plates you would say:

O-sara ni-mai kudasai. (*Oh-Sah-rah nee-my kuu-dah-sie*)

O-sara means plate or plates, **ni** means two; **mai** refers to flat things; and **kudasai** means please give me/us or bring me/us... Three plates would be **o-sara san-mai** (*Oh-sah-rah sahn-my*); four plates, **o-sara yon-mai** (*Oh-sah-rah yoan-my*), etc.

The numerative for small round things like bottles of beer, for example, is **hon** (*hoan*)—sometimes pronounced as *bone*.

Example: Two bottles of beer, please.

Biru ni-hon kudasai. (*Bee-ruu nee-hoan kuu-dah-sie*).

Following are some of the other common numeratives:

Satsu (*sot-sue*) for books.

Fukuro (*fuu-kuu-roe*) for bags or things shaped like bags.

Kire (*kee-ray*) for slices of things like meat and bread.

Two books: **hon ni-satsu** (*hoan nee-sot-sue*)

Three slices of bread:
pan san-kire (*pahn sahn-kee-ray*)

Note that in Japanese the number and numerative follow the object mentioned:

Two pencils: **enpitsu ni-hon** (*en-peet-sue nee-hoan*).

Five sheets of paper: **kami go-mai** (*kah-me go-my*).

When counting or ordering something like hamburgers, which have a more or less indefinite shape, it is common to use the Japanese set of numerals.

Two hamburgers, please.
Hanbaga wo futatsu kudasai.
(*Hahn-bah-gah oh fuu-tot-sue kuu-dah-sie.*)

In numbering and counting from ten on you use only the Chinese set of numerals, which makes things a lot easier. And from 11 to 99 the numbers follow a very simple pattern.

11 is **ju-ichi** (*juu-ee-chee*), or 10 plus 1
12 is **ju-ni** (*juu-nee*), or 10 plus 2
15 is **ju-go** (*juu-go*), or 10 plus 5

20 is **ni-ju** (*nee-juu*), or two tens
21 is **ni-ju-ichi** (*nee-juu-ee-chee*), or two tens plus 1
22 is **ni-ju-ni** (*nee-juu-nee*), or two tens plus 2

30 is **san ju** (*sahn-juu*), or three tens
31 is **san-ju-ichi** (*sahn-juu-ee-chee*), or three tens plus 1

40 is **yon-ju** (*yoan-juu*), or four tens
41 is **yon-ju-ichi** (*yoan-juu-ee-chee*), or four tens plus 1

This pattern continues through 99: **kyu-ju-kyu** (*cue-juu-cue*), or nine tens plus nine.

The word for 100 is **hyaku** (*h'yah-kuu*), and the same pattern continues:

101 is **hyaku-ichi** (*h'yah-kuu ee-chee*), or 100 plus 1
105 is **hyaku-go** (*h'yah-kuu-go*), or 100 plus 5
199 is **hyaku kyu-ju-kyu** (*h'yah-kuu cue-ju-cue*), or 100 plus 99.
200 is **ni-hyaku** (*nee-h'yah-kuu*), or two 100s.

When you come to 300 there is a slight change in the pronunciation of **hyaku**. It becomes **byaku** (*b'yah-kuu*), which is easier to pronounce.

In other words, 300 is **san-byaku** (*sahn-b'yah-kuu*).
301 is **san-byaku-ichi** (*sahn-b'yah-ku-ee-chee*).
400 is **yon-hyaku** (*yoan b'yah-kuu*)
500 is **go-hyaku** (*go-b'yah-kuu*)

And there are new words for 1,000 **sen** (*sen*); and 10,000: **man** (*mahn*).

10,000 is **ichi-man** (*ee-chee mahn*); 20,000 is **ni-man** (*nee-mahn*).

Here is a more complete listing:

11 **juichi** (*juu-ee-chee*)
12 **juni** (*juu-nee*)
13 **jusan** (*juu-sahn*)
14 **juyon** (*juu-yoan*); also: **jushi** (*juu-she*)
15 **jugo** (*juu-go*)
16 **juroku** (*juu-roe-kuu*)
17 **jushichi** (*juu-she-chee*)
18 **juhachi** (*juu-hah-chee*)
19 **jukyu** (*juu-cue*); also: **juku** (*juu-kuu*)

20 **niju** (*neejuu*)
21 **nijuichi** (*nee-juu-ee-chee*)
22 **nijuni** (*nee-juu-nee*)
23 **nijusan** (*nee-juu-sahn*)
24 **nijushi** (*nee-juu-she*)
25 **nijugo** (*nee-juu-go*)
30 **sanju** (*sahn-juu*)
31 **sanju-ichi** (*sahn-juu-ee-chee*)

40 **yonju** (*yoan-juu*)
50 **goju** (*go-juu*)
60 **rokuju** (*roe-kuu-juu*)
70 **nanaju** (*nah-nah-juu*); also: **shichiju** (*she-chee-juu*)
80 **hachiju** (*hah-chee-juu*)
90 **kyuju** (*cue-juu*)

100 **hyaku** (*h'yah-kuu*)
101 **hyaku-ichi** (*h'yah-kuu-ee-chee*)
102 **hyaku-ni** (*h'yah-kuu-nee*)
110 **hyaku-ju** (*h'yah-kuu-juu*)
110 **hyaku-juichi** (*h'yah-kuu-juu-ee-chee*)
120 **hyaku-niju** (*h'yah-kuu-nee-juu*)
130 **hyaku-sanju** (*h'yah-kuu-sahn-juu*)
150 **hyaku-goju** (*h'yah-kuu-go-juu*)

200 **nihyaku** (*nee-h'yah-kuu*)
300 **sanbyaku** (*sahn-b'yah-kuu*)
400 **yonhyaku** (*yoan-h'yah-kuu*)
500 **gohyaku** (*go-h'yah-kuu*)
600 **roppyaku** (*roe-p'yah-kuu*)
700 **nanahyaku** (*nah-nah-h'yah-kuu*)
800 **happyaku** (*hop-p'yah-kuu*)
900 **kyuhyaku** (*k'yuu-h'yah-kuu*)

1,000 **sen** *(sen)*; **issen** (*ees-sen*)
1,500 **sen-gohyaku** (*sen-go-h'yah-kuu*)
2,000 **nisen** (*nee-sen*)
2,700 **nisen-nanahyaku** (*nee-sen-nah-nah-h'yah-kuu*)
2,900 **nisen-kyuhyaku** (*nee-sen-cue-h'yah-kuu*)

3,000 **sanzen** (*sahn-zen*)
4,000 **yonsen** (*yoan-sen*)
5,000 **gosen** (*go-sen*)
9,000 **kyusen** (*cue-sen*)
10,000 **ichiman** (*ee-chee-mahn*)
11,000 **ichiman-issen** (*ee-chee-mahn-ee-sen*)
12,000 **ichiman-nisen** (*ee-chee-mahn-nee-sen*)
15,000 **ichiman-gosen** (*ee-chee-mahn-go-sen*)
20,000 **niman** (*nee-mahn*)
25,000 **niman-gosen** (*nee-mahn-go-sen*)
50,000 **goman** (*go-mahn*)
100,000 **juman** (*juu-mahn*)

This numbering system may appear daunting but rarely presents a big problem. Do not worry too much about following it precisely. If you do not know the correct numerative for what you want, just use numbers from either of the two sets. In an emergency you can always resort to hand signs or paper and pencil. All Japanese can read Arabic numbers.

General Shopping Vocabulary

Following is a list of words and phrases you will find useful when shopping in Japan. Note that in Japanese there is no distinction between the singular and plural; the number is understood from the context. For example, **kutsu** (*koot-sue*) can mean shoe or shoes.

Advance payment **saki-barai** (*sah-kee-bah-rie*)

Should I pay in advance?
Saki-barai desu ka? (*Sah-kee-bah-rie dess kah?*)

Advertised special
kukoku no shina (*koe-koe-kuu no she-nah*)

Where are the advertised specials?
Kokoku no shina wa doko desu ka?
(*Koe-koe-kuu no she-nah wah doe-koe dess kah?*)

Bargain **okai-doku** (*oh-kie-doe-kuu*);
also: **baagen** (*baah-gane*)

Bargain floor
moyoshi-mono kaijo (*moe-yoe-she-moe-no kie-joe*).

Which floor is the bargain floor?
Moyoshi-mono kaijo wa nan kai desu ka?
(*Moe-yoe-she-moe-no kiejoe wah nahn kie dess kah?*)

bargain goods **okai-doku-hin** (*oh-kie-doe-kuu-heen*)

bargain sale **baagen seru** (*baah-gane say-rue*)

When does the sale start?
Baagen seru wa itsu kara desu ka?
(*Baah-gen say-rue wah eet-sue kah-rah dess kah?*)

Big **okii** (*oh-kee*)

These shoes are big. **Kono kutsu wa okii desu.**
(*Koe-no kuut-sue wah oh-kee dess.*)

Bigger **motto o kii** (*mote-toe oh-kee*)

Let me see a bigger one.
Motto okii no wo misete kudasai.
(*Mote-toe oh-ee no oh me-say-tay kuu-dah-sie.*)

Black **kuroi** (*kuu-roy*)

Do you have black ones? **Kuroi no ga arimasu ka?**
(*Kuu-roy no gah ah-ree-mahss-kah?*)

Blue **aoi** (*ah-oh-ee*); also: **buru** (*buu-rue*)

I like blue. **Buru ga suki desu.** (*Buu-rue gah ski dess.*)

Bright; loud **hade-na** (*hah-day-nah*)

I don't want anything loud.
Hade-na mono wa hoshiku arimasen.
(*Hah-day-nah moe-no wah hoe-she-kuu ah-ree-mah-sen.*)

Brown **cha-iro** (*chah-ee-roe*)

Do you have brown socks?
Cha-iro no kutsu-shita ga arimasu ka?
(*Chah-ee-roe no kuut-sue-ssh-tah gah ah-ree-mahss kah?*)

budget **yosan** (*yoe-sahn*)

I'm over my budget.
Yosan ga mo nakunarimashita.
(*Yoe-sahn gab moe nah-kuu-nah-ree-mah-sshtah.*)

Change (money) **o-tsuri** (*oh-t'sue-ree*);
also: **chenji** (*chane-jee*)

I forgot my change. **O-tsuri wo wasuremashita.**
(*Oh-t'sue-ree oh wah-sue-ray-mah-sshtah.*)

Cheap **yasui** (*yah-sue-e*)

Too expensive **taka sugiru** (*tah-kah sue-ghee-rue*)

Cheaper **motto yasui** (*mote-toe yah-sue-e*)

Fashionable **ryuko no** (*r'yuu-koe no*)

Clearance Sale **zaiko isso seru** (*zie-koe ee-soe say-rue*)

Final Clearance Sale
saishu shobun (*sie-show show-buun*)

Clothing (Western) **yofuku** (*yoe-fuu-kuu*)

Clothing store **yofuku-ya** (*yoe-fuu-kuu-yah*)

Coupon **sabisu-ken** (*sah-bee-sue-ken*); also:
shoppingu chiketto (*shope-peen-guu chee-ket-toe*)

Dark **kurai** (*kuu-rye*)

Deliver **haitatsu shimasu** (*hie-tot-sue she-mahss*); also:
todokemasu (*toe-doe-kay-mahss*)

Please deliver it.
Todokete kudasai. (*Toe-doe-kay-tay kuu-dah-sie.*)

Department store **depato** (*day-pah-toe*)

Discount **disukaunto** (*dis-koun-toe*);
also: **waribiki** (*wah-ree-beekee*)

Will you discount (it)?
Waribiki shite kuremasu ka?
(*Wah-ree-bee-kee ssh-tay kuu-ray-mahss kah?*)

Disposable **tsukai-sute** (*t'sky-sue-tay*)

Duty-Free item **menzei-hin** (*men-zay-e-heen*)

Is this a duty-free item?
Kore wa menzei-hin desu ka?
(*Koe-ray wah men-zay-e-heen dess kah?*)

Elegant **johin-na** (*joe-heen-nah*)

End-of-the-Year Gift **O'seibu** (*oh-say-e-boe*)

Everything; all **zenpin** (*zen-peen*);
also: **zenbu** (*zen-buu*)

Exchange (merchandise)
tori-kaemasu (*toe-ree-kie-mahss*)

I would like to exchange this.
Kore wo tori-kaetai desu.
(*Koe-ray oh toe-ree-kie-tie dess.*)

Expensive **takai** (*tah-kie*)

Fish market **uo ichiba** (*uu-oh ee-chee-bah*)

Folk craft **mingei-hin** (*meen-gay-e-heen*)

Furniture **kagu** (*kah-guu*)

Genuine **honmono** (*hoan-moe-no*)

Is this genuine leather?
Kore wa honmono no kawa desu ka?
(*Koe-ray wah hoan-moe-no no kah-wah dess kah?*)

Gift **okuri-mono** (*oh-kuu-ree-moe-no*);
also: **miyage** (*me-yah-gay*); **gifuto** (*gheef-toe*)

It's a gift so please wrap it up.
Gifuto desu kara tsutsunde kudasai.
(*Gheef-toe dess kah-rah t'sue-t'sune-day kuu-dah-sie.*)

Gold (color) **kin-iro** (*keen-ee-roe*)

Gram **guramu** (*guu-rah-muu*)

Green **gurin** (*guu-reen*); also: **midori** (*me-doe-ree*)

Grocery store **shokuhin-ten** (*show-kuu-heen-ten*)

Guarantee card **hosho-sho** (*hoe-show-show*)

Half price **hangaku** (*hahn-gah-kuu*)

Handmade **tezukuri** (*tay-zuu-kuu-ree*)

Is that handmade? **Sore wa tezukuri desu ka?**
(*Soe-ray wah tay zuu-kuu-ree dess kah?*)

Hard **katai** (*kah-tie*)

Heavy **omoi** (*oh-moy*)

Height (of a person) **shincho** (*sheen-choe*)

Imitation **mozo-hin** (*moe-zoe-heen*);
also **nisemono** (*nee-say-moe-no*)

That looks like an imitation.
Sore wa mozo-hin no yo desu.
(*Soe-ray wah moe-zoe-heen no yoe dess.*)

Imported goods **yunyu-hin** (*yuun-yuu-heen*)

Do you carry imported goods?
Yunyuhin wo oite imasu ka?
(*Yuun-yuu-heen oh oh-ee-tay ee-mahss kah?*)

Large **okii** (*oh-kee*)

Last of the stock
genpin kagiri (*gane-peen kah-ghee-ree*)

Light color **akarui iro** (*ah-kah-ruu-e ee-roe*)

Lightweight **karui** (*kah-ruu-ee*)

List price **teika** (*tay-ee-kah*)

Local specialty **meisan** (*may-ee-sahn*);
also **meibutsu** (*may-ee-boot-sue*)

I want to buy a local specialty.
Meibutsu wo kaitai desu.
(*May-ee-boot-sue oh kie-tie dess.*)

Made-in-Japan **Nihon-Sei** (*Nee-hoan-Say-ee*)

Was this made in Japan?
Kore wa Nihon-Sei desu ka?
(*Koe-ray wah Nee-hoan-Say-ee dess kah?*)

Manual of instructions
Setsumei-sho (*Sate-sue-may-ee show*)

Market **ichiba** (*ee-chee-bah*)

Midsummeer gift **Ochugen** (*Oh-chuu-gane*)

Money **Okane** (*Oh-kah-nay*)

Money Exchange **Ryo-Gae** (*rio-guy*)

Newly on sale **shin hatsubai** (*sheen hot-sue-by*)

Open (for business) **kaiten** (*kie-tane*)

Plain, conservative **jimi-na** (*jee-me-nah*)

Let me see something a little more conservative.
Mo sukoshi jimi-na mono wo misete kudasai. (*Moe suu-koe-shee jee-me-nah moe-no oh me-say-tay kuu-dah-sie.*)

Premium giveaway **keihin** (*kay-ee-heen*)

Present (gift) **omiyage** (*oh-me-yah-gay*)

Price **nedan** (*nay-dahn*)

Price tag **sho fuda** (*show-fuu-dah*),
also **ne fuda** (*nay-fuu-dah*)

Quality **hinshitsu** (*heen sheet-sue*)

Do you have one that is better quality?
Motto ii hinshitsu no ga arimasu ka?
(*Moat-toe ee heen-sheet-sue no gah ah-ree-mahss kah?*)

Receipt **ryoshu-sho** (*rio-shuu-show*)

Please give me a receipt. **Ryoshusho wo kudasai.**
(*Rio-shuu-show oh kuu-dah-sie*)

Red **akai** (*ah-kie*)

Reduced price **nesage** (*nay-sah-gay*)

Sample **mihon** (*me-hone*)

Secondhand store
chukohin ten (*chuu-koe-heen tane*)

Are there any secondhand stores near here?
Kono chikaku ni chukohin ten arimasu ka? (*Koe-no chee-kah-kuu nee chuu-koe-heen tane ah-ree-mahss kah?*)

Send (as by mail) **okurimasu** (*oh-kuu-ree-mahss*)

Shopping mall/shopping street
meiten-gai (*may-ee-tane guy*)

Silver (color) **gin iro** (*ghee nee-roe*)

Small **chiisai** (*cheee-sie*)

Smaller **motto chiisai** (*moat-toe cheee-sie*)

I need a smaller size.
Motto chiisai saizu ga irimasu.
(*Moat-toe cheee-sie sie-zuu gah ee-ree-mahss.*)

Sold out **uri-kire** (*uu-ree-kee-ree*)

Souvenir **kinen-hin** (*kee-nane-heen*);
also **omiyage** (*oh-me-yah-gay*)

Special order
tokubetsu chumon (*toe-kuu-bate-suu chuu-moan*)

Special price **tokka** (*toke-kah*)

Special sale **tokubai** (*toe-kuu-by*)

Specialty store **senmon ten** (*sen-moan-tane*)

Supermarket **supa** (*suu-pah*)

Super special price **cho tokka** (*choh toke-kah*)

Today only **honjitsu kagiri** (*hoan-jeet-sue kah-ghee-ree*)

Underground shopping area **chika-gai** (*chee-kah-guy*)

Where is the nearest underground shopping center?
Ichiban chikai chika-gai wa doko desu ka? (*Ee-chee-bahn chee-kie chee-kah-guy wah doe-koe dess kah?*)

White **shiroi** (*she-roy*)

Wrap **tsutsumimasu** (*t'sue-t'sue-me-mahss*)

Wrapping paper **tsutsumi gami** (*t'sue-t'sue-me gah-me*)

Written instructions **setsumei-sho** (*sate-sue-may-show*)

Do you have instructions in English?
Eibun no setsumei-sho ga arimasu ka?
(*Aa-ee-buun no sate-sue-may-show ah-ree-mahss kah?*)

CHAPTER 4

Product Information

Most Japanese products that require information about their use are accompanied by instruction sheets or pamphlets called **setsumei-sho** (*set-sue-may-e-show*).

Products intended for export and for sale to tourists are accompanied by instruction materials in English and sometimes in other foreign languages. Merchandise intended for sale in Japan usually comes with instructions in Japanese only.

The Metric System

The metric system is commonly used for measurements in Japan. Following are metric and American equivalents for some of the more common measurements:

Length:
    1 inch = 2.54 centimeters
    1 centimeter = 0.394 inch
    1 foot = 0.305 meter
    1 meter = 3.281 feet
    1 yard = 0.914 meter
    1 meter = 1.094 yards
    1 mile = 1.609 kilometers
    1 kilometer = 0.621 mile

Area:
> 1 square inch = 6.451 square centimeters
> 1 square centimeter = 0.155 square inch
> 1 square foot = 0.093 square meter
> 1 square meter = 1.196 square yards
> 1 square yard = 0.836 square meter

Volume:
> 1 cubic inch = 16.387 cubic centimeters
> 1 cubic centimeter = 0.061 cubic inch
> 1 cubic foot = 0.028 cubic meter
> 1 cubic meter = 1.308 cubic yards
> 1 cubic yard = 0.765 cubic meter

Weight:
> 1 ounce = 28.349 grams
> 100 grams = 0.220 pound
> 1 pound = 0.453 kilogram
> 1 kilogram = 2.20 pounds

Liquid:
> 1 ounce = 29.573 milliliters
> 1 liter = 2.113 pints
> 1 pint = 0.473 liter
> 1 liter = 0.264 gallon
> 1 quart = 0.946 liter
> 1 gallon = 3.785 liters

Finding Your Japanese Size

Clothing and shoe sizes in Japan are based on the metric system and a traditional Japanese numerical system. Learning and remembering the Japanese equivalents of your size can be daunting and confusing, and there is no need to try.

Apparel and shoe stores that are patronized by foreign residents and visitors have comparison charts for comparable United States, United Kingdom, and continental European sizes.

If you are in a store that does not have the appropriate charts, or the comparison charts fail, the alternative, of course, is to try things on—which most people do anyway.

Women's suits and blouses are in sizes 5, 7, 9, 11, 13, and 15. An average-sized Japanese woman takes size 9. Clothes may also be marked S, M, L and XL, where M is the Japanese average. Men's shirts often show the collar size and sleeve length in centimeters. Shoe sizes are also in centimeters.

CHAPTER 5

Consumption Taxes
税金
Zeikin (*Zay-ee-keen*)

As previously noted, Japan has a consumption sales tax of 5 percent on all consumer products, restaurant tabs, transportation fees, sightseeing charges, and hotel accommodations. Additional "local taxes" of 3 percent are applied in some areas when a purchase exceeds a fixed figure.

For hotel accommodations, there is a flat tax of 5 percent on all room charges up to ¥10,000 and a surcharge on room charges over ¥10,000. First-class and international hotels may add a service charge—usually 15 percent—to their bills.

On restaurant bills, the tax is 5 percent on charges under ¥5,000 and a small surcharge on bills totaling ¥5,000 and over. A flat tax of 5 percent is assessed on all air-and long-distance transportation services and on the cost of sightseeing tours.

There are so many variations in taxes in Japan that it is virtually impossible to keep them in mind, so it is better not to try. The only sensible recourse is to inquire about applicable taxes before making a purchase. Major increases in taxation occurred in 2002—and additional increases are on the government agenda.

Purchases in duty-free and tax-free shops are not taxed. Airport limousine bus fares are also tax-free. Some shops and other businesses include the taxes in their listed prices to make it easier for themselves as well as their patrons.

CHAPTER 6

Major Shopping Meccas
in Tokyo

There are probably more than a thousand shopping areas in Tokyo (I don't believe anyone has ever counted them!). To begin with, Tokyo grew up from some 300 villages and residential areas—all of which had their own shopping centers.

Now there are at least a thousand recognizable communities in the sprawling city, most of which have their own **shotengai** (*show-tane-guy*) or "shopping street." Then all of the major commuter train and subway stations in the city are surrounded by shopping and dining facilities—many of which are as large and as comprehensive as individual cities. These centers alone add up to more than 100.

That said, the largest and most popular shopping areas in Tokyo are the famous **Ginza** noted for its upscale boutiques and department stores, the equally famous **Akihabara** district with its hundreds of electric and electronic product shops [over 250 at the last count], the **Hibiya-Yurakucho** area which adjoins the Ginza on the west, the new Omotesando Boulevard area between **Aoyama** and **Harajuku**, the "downtown" areas of **Shibuya** and **Shinjuku** which are cities within themselves, and **Nihonbashi**—the latter known for its department stores (Mitsukoshi and Takashimaya).

Other major shopping areas in the city that are primarily frequented by residents include **Asakusa**, **Akasaka**, **Aoyama**, **Roppongi**, **Ueno**, **Okachimachi**, **Kanda**, and **Ikebukuro**.

All of these centers are amply served by subway lines, making them easily accessible from virtually any hotel in Tokyo.

CHAPTER 7

Antique Shops
骨董屋
Kotto-Ya (*Kote-toe-Yah*)

All major cities in Japan have several well-known antique shops, **kotto-ya** (*kote-toe-yah*). Some of these shops also sell old art objects, or **kogei-hin** (*koe-gay-heen*).

Popular products include lacquered tables, trays, bowls and boxes, porcelain and pottery, iron objects, stoneware and woodblock prints.

Virtually all of the old handicraft products available in antique shops are still being made by today's craftsmen, and can be found in specialty shops, in department stores, and in shops catering to foreign visitors like the Oriental Bazaar in Harajuku in Tokyo.

The best buys for antiques are usually found in antique shops away from downtown areas of large cities, in provincial towns and cities, and most often in the same towns and cities where the products have been made for centuries.

If time and other constraints prevent you from seeking out these sources, your best bet is to shop at stores that collect such items from the countryside and advertise themselves to foreign visitors in the various local media. Following are some of the better known antique shops in Tokyo:

Akari-ya, 8-1, 4-chome, Yoyogi, Shibuya-ku (near Sangubashi Station on the Odakyu Line from Shin juku). Tel. 3465–5578. Hours: 11 a.m. to 7 p.m. except

Sundays and holidays. Specialties: chests, Imari chinaware, screens, bronzes. A branch shop, Akari-ya II, a short distance south of the main shop, features rare Japanese textiles, including old kimono and sashes.

Art Plaza Magatani, 10-3, 5-chome, Toranomon, Minato-ku (just south of Kamiyacho Station on the Hibiya Line, next to a Shinto shrine). Tel. 3433–6321. Hours: 10 a.m. to 7 p.m. Specialties: chinaware, scrolls, lacquerware.

Edo Antiques, 2–21–12 Akasaka, Minato-ku (off the main Tameike-Roppongi thoroughfare near the small Hotel Tokyu Kanko). Tel. 3584–5280. Hours: 10 a.m. to 6 p.m. except Sundays. Specialties: chests, ceramics, kimono, sashes, lacquerware.

Fuso Oriental Arts & Curios, 7–647 Akasaka, Minato-ku (first floor of Akasaka New Plaza, near Akasaka Station on the Chiyoda Line). Tel. 3583–5945. Hours: 10 a.m. to 6 p.m. except Sundays.

Geishinsha, 3rd fl., Sanyo bldg., 8–10, l-chome, Kyobashi, Chuo-ku.

Hanabishi, New Melsa bldg., 6–19, 6-chome, Ginza, Chuo-ku.

Hasebe-ya, 5–24, l-chome, Azabujuban, Minato-ku. Tel. 3401–9998/8840.

Hatoya, 5–14, 6-chome, Ginza, Chuo-ku.

Honjo Gallery, 1–6, 6-chome, Minami Aoyama, Minato-ku. Tel. 3400–0277/0278.

Maruyama, 5–9, 2-chome, Kyobashi, Chuo-ku.

Oriental Bazaar, 9–13, 5-chome, Meiji Jingumae, Shibuya-ku. (Several individual shops in one multi-story building; with overseas shipping services.)

Toraya, 13–1, 5-chome, Minami Aoyama, Minato-ku.

Yokoyama, 2nd fl., Sukiyabashi Shopping Center, 1, 5-chome, Ginza. Also Hilton Hotel arcade and Hotel Okura arcade. This shop was established in 1895 in Kyoto, where the main shop is still located.

Antiques Vocabulary

Antiques and curios are special categories, so having some knowledge of the vocabulary can be very helpful.

Armor **yoroi** (*yoe-roe-ee*)

Bamboo and oilpaper umbrellas
ban-gasa (*bahn-gah-sah*);
also **janome-gasa** (*jah-no-may-gah-sah*)

Calligraphy **sho** (*show*)

Candleholders **rosoku-tate** (*roe-soe-kuu-tah-tay*)

Carvings **chokoku** (*choe-koe-kuu*)

Ceramic ware **seto-mono** (*say-toe-moe-no*)

Chests of drawers **tansu** (*tahn-sue*)

Clothes boxes **tsuzura** (*tsue-zoo-rah*)

Curios **kotto-hin** (*kote-toe-heen*)

Damascene **damashin** (*dah-mah-sheen*)

Dolls **ningyo** (*neen-g'yoe*)

Earthenware **tsubo** (*t'sue-boe*)

Embroidery **shishu** (*she-shuu*)

Fans (dance) **mai ogi** (*my oh-ghee*)

Fans (folding) **sensu** (*sen-sue*)

Fans (round) **uchiwa** (*uu-chee-wah*)

"Foating world" pictures **ukiyo-e** (*uu-kee-yoe-eh*)

Flower vases **kabin** (*kah-bean*)

Folk crafts **mingei-hin** (*meen-gay-e-heen*)

Hanging scrolls **kakejiku** (*kah-kay-jee-kuu*);
also: **kake-mono** (*kah-kay-moe-no*)

Helmets **kabuto** (*kah-buu-toe*)

India ink painting **sumi-e** (*sue-me-eh*)

Japanese paintings **nihon-ga** (*nee-hoan-gah*)

Jewelry boxes **hoseki-bako** (*hoe-say-kee-bah-koe*)

Lacquerware **nuri-mono** (*nuu-ree-moe-no*);
also: **shikki** (*she-kee*)

Lamps **ranpu** (*rahn-puu*)

Masks **men** (*men*)

Music boxa **orugoru** (*oh-rue-go-rue*)

Old coins **kosen** (*koe-sen*)

Ornaments; knick-knacks
kazari-mono (*kah-zah-ree-moe-no*)

Picture frames **gaku-buchi** (*gah-kuu-buu-chee*)

Pottery **toki** (*toe-kee*); also: **togei** (*toe-gay-ee*)

Replicas; reproductions **fukusei** (*fuu-kuu-say-ee*)

Swords **katana** (*kah-tah-nah*); also: **token** (*toe-ken*)

Tapestries **kabe-kake** (*kah-bay-kah-kay*)

CHAPTER 8

Apparel Stores
洋服屋
Yofuku-ya (*Yoe-fuu-kuu-yah*)

Buying ready-made apparel in Japan is a problem for many foreigners because they are bigger than most Japanese. For those with petite, small, or medium-sized builds, however, there are vast choices in fabrics and styles, ranging from funky to high fashion.

A number of Japanese fashion designers are now world famous and have created multinational empires.

Japan's leading department stores devote a substantial amount of space to apparel, from sportswear to evening wear. The center for Japan's fashion world is the Harayuku-Aoyama area of Tokyo. Many top designers and most of the larger apparel manufacturers have offices and outlets in this area.

In Tokyo you can get a good overview of apparel in Japan by visiting shops and factory outlets along **Omotesando** and **Meiji boulevards** in Harajuku, and in the 5-chome section of Aoyama Boulevard.

For those who like funky clothing, the place to go is **Takeshita-dori**, which begins in front of the small north exit of Harajuku Station and goes down the slope, connecting with Meiji Boulevard about four blocks away.

Virtually all of the world's top fashion brands are in Japan—with the sizes scaled-down for the Japanese, and in some cases the overall look adapted to the Japanese taste.

Banana Republic may not qualify as a boutique shop, but **Gap** (Japan), the Japanese arm of the United States parent company, opened its flagship shop on the Ginza in 2005, along with branch shops in upscale **Coredor Nihonbashi** and **Roppongi Hills** in Tokyo, and a shop in Yokohama.

(Prior to the opening of the stores, the styles of the popular Banana Republic lines of merchandise were also altered to "fit Japanese taste.")

In the meantime, the Japanese kimono and the casual **yukata**/*yuu-kah-tah* (robe) have made a comeback. Kimono are worn for a wide variety of occasions, from tea ceremonies to festivals.

Yukata are provided for virtually all inn and hotel guests in Japan, and are the uniform-of-the-day in hotspring resorts and other vacation areas. **Yukata** and **happi** (*hop-pee*) jackets are high on the shopping lists of international visitors.

CHAPTER 9

Art Galleries
ギャラリー
Gyarari (*G'yah-rah-ree*)

Shopping for fine art in Japan is probably limited to people specifically interested in Japanese artists because fine-art objects have become very expensive.

However, the works of some very good Japanese painters are available for less than astronomical prices because they are more appreciated abroad than they are at home, and the value of their work has not been artificially inflated.

One very convenient feature of the world of Japanese art is the country's network of leading department stores, which often have their own galleries, and regularly sponsor work by deserving artists. Large department stores with their own galleries include Daimaru, Isetan, Keio, Mitsukoshi, Takashimaya, Odakyu, Seibu, and Tokyu.

Other galleries in Tokyo where you can see the work of Japanese artists include the following:

Gallery Mikimoto, 5–5, 4-chome, Ginza, Chuo-ku

Ginzado Gallery, 2–13, 3-chome, Ginza, Chuo-ku

Nichido Gallery, 4–12, 7-chome, Ginza, Chuo-ku

Shiseido Gallery, 8–3, 8-chome, Ginza, Chuo-ku

Yoseido Gallery, 5–15, 5- chome, Ginza, Chuo-ku

Fine-arts Vocabulary

Art **geijutsu** (*gay-e-jute-sue*)

Art exhibit **bijutsu-ten** (*bee-jute-sue-ten*)

Artist **geijutsu-ka** (*gay-e-jute-sue-kah*);
also: **bijutsu-ka** (*bee-jute-sue-kah*)

Canvas **kanbasu** (*kahn-bahss*)

Exhibit **tenran-kai** (*ten-rahn-kie*)

Fine-arts gallery **bijutsu-kan** (*bee-jute-sue-kahn*)

"Foating world" pictures **ukiyo-e** (*uu-kee-yoe-eh*)

Frame **gaku-buchi** (*gah-kuu-buu-chee*)

Gallery **gyarari** (*g'yah-rah-ree*)

Japanese painting **nihon-ga** (*nee-hoan-gah*)

Oil painting **abura-e** (*ah-buu-rah-eh*)

Painter **e-kaki** (*eh-kah-kee*); also: **gaka** (*gah-kah*)

Painting **e** (*eh*)

Photograph **shashin** (*shah-sheen*)

Photographer **kamera-man** (*kah-may-rah-mahn*); also:
shashin-ka (*shah-sheen-kah*)

Portrait **jinbutsu-ga** (*jeen-buut-sue-gah*)

Showing **tenran-kai** (*ten-rahn-kie*)

Signature **shomei** (*show-may-e*)

Still life **seibutsu-ga** (*say-ee-buut-sue-gah*)

Watercolor **suisai-ga** (*sue-e-sie-gah*)

Western painting **yo-ga** (*yoe-gah*)

Woodblock print **mokuhan-ga** (*moe-kuu-hahn-gah*)

CHAPTER 10

Bakeries
パン屋
Pan-ya (*Pahn-yah*)

Japan's bakeries are one of the delights of the country—a remarkable surprise for many because the popular image of the country has always been that of a rice country rather than a bread country. But as in so many other areas, the Japanese have assimilated bread into their culture, just as they have Western apparel, household furnishings, hobbies, and Western entertainment.

Bakeries are found in neighborhood and central shopping districts, in commuter-terminal shopping areas, in department stores and supermarkets, even in some hotels. Like their French counterparts, Japanese bakeries turn out daily a variety of breads and rolls to fit practically every taste. Many specialize in single servings of pastries, with toppings and fillings like baked apple and sweetened chestnut. Primarily consumed as snacks, these attractive pastries are also popular as gifts for home visits and treats for fellow workers.

In addition to thousands of independent bakeries there are several bakery chains in Japan, including **Kimuraya**, **Nakamuraya** and **Yamazaki**.

Tourists who are traveling on budgets almost always discover Japan's amazing bakery world, and take full advantage of it. Others might want to sample some of the unusual breads and pastries just for the special delight.

There are several dozens of bakery chains in Japan, including **Saint-germain**, **Kimura-ya**, **Andersen**, **DONQ** and **Doughnut Plant**.

Bakery Vocabulary

bagel **beguru** (*bay-guu-rue*)

black bread **kuro-pan** (*kuu-roe-pahn*)

bread **pan** (*pahn*)

cake **keki** (*kay-kee*)

cornbread **kon-bureddo** (*kone-buu-ray-doe*)

croissant **kurowassan** (*kuu-roe-wahs-san*)

donut **donatsu** (*doe-not-sue*)

French bread **Furansu-pan** (*fuu-rahn-sue-pahn*)

French roll **Furenchi-roru** (*fuu-ren-chee-roe-rue*)

German bread **Doitsu-pan** (*doe-eet-sue-pahn*)

muffin **mafin** (*mah-feen*)

pastry **pesutori** (*pay-sue-toe-ree*)

raisin bread **budo-pan** (*buu-doe-pahn*)

roll **roru-pan** (*roe-rue-pahn*)

rye bread **rai-mugi-pan** (*rie-muu-ghee-pahn*)

walnut bread **kurumi-pan** (*kuu-ruu-me-pahn*)

white bread **shoku-pan** (*show-kuu-pahn*)

CHAPTER 11

Bookstores
本屋
Honya (*Hone-yah*)

Japan is one of the great book-publishing centers of the world, with a network of bookstores and other book outlets that are unsurpassed.

This phenomenon started in the 1870s and 80s when the post-Shogunate government began a crash program to import Western learning enmasse into the country through both books and foreign teachers.

In the following decades more translations and publication of foreign books took place in Japan than had ever occurred before in history, and this pace has continued. Still today no other country imports, translates and publishes as many foreign books as Japan.

In addition to the large number of Japanese publishing companies, dozens of major American and European publishers have branches in Japan.

The oldest and best-known of the foreign publishers in Japan is the Tuttle Publishing Company, founded in Tokyo in 1948 by Charles E. Tuttle, a Vermont United States native whose family had been in the publishing business for several generations. Tuttle Publishing is now a member of the Periplus Publishing Group, which has editorial offices and distribution centers in Singapore, Japan and the United States.

Most of Japan's international hotels have bookstores that cater specifically to tourists and visiting businessmen. In addition to travel guides, language books, and general titles on Japan, hotel bookshops usually carry selections of bestsellers from the United States and other countries.

Two major Japanese bookstore chains, **Maruzen** and **Kinokuniya**, specialize in imported books in foreign languages, especially English, as well as locally published English-language books on Japan.

Maruzen's main Tokyo branch, said to be the largest foreign language bookstore in the country, is catty-cornered across from the northwest corner of Tokyo Station in the rather spectacular 18-story Oazo Building. It takes up four floors of the building. English language titles are on the 4th floor.

Kinokuniya's main Tokyo shop adjoins the southeast corner of the Shinjuku Station complex in Takashimaya Times Square. It takes up several floors in a large free-standing building on the south side of the square.

Dozens of smaller bookstore chains and thousands of independent shops throughout the country carry selections of books in English. And there are bookshops (and shops with a selection of books) in the arrival and departure areas of the International airports.

A few drugstores patronized by foreign residents and visitors, including the American Pharmacy in the Marunouchi Building (in front of Tokyo Station) also carry a small selection of books.

Japan's biggest concentration of bookstores, selling new and used books, is in the Jimbocho/Kanda district of Chiyoda ward, a short distance north of the Imperial Palace grounds in central Tokyo. The Hanzomon and Toei Shinjuku subway lines have a Jimbocho/Kanda Station.

Many of the country's top publishing houses have their own shops in this area. The two largest literary agencies in Japan, the Tuttle-Mori Agency and Japan Uni Agency, are also located in Kanda's Jimbocho district.

Many large railway stations (such as Shinagawa in Tokyo) also have bookstores on their premises.

See the *Japan Yellow Pages*, and local English-language telephone directories for an extensive list of bookshops carrying English-language books.

Book Vocabulary

author **sakka** (*sahk-kah*), also **chosha** (*choe-shah*)

book **hon** (*hoan*)

bookshelf **hon-dana** (*hoan-dah-nah*)

bookstore **hon-ya** (*hoan-yah*)

dictionary **jibiki** (*gee-bee-kee*), also **jisho** (*jee-show*)

English-Japanese dictionary
Ei-Wa jiten (*aa-ee-wah-jee-ten*)

Japanese-English dictionary
Wa-Ei jiten (*wah-aa-ee jee-ten*)

distributor (wholesaler) **toritsugi** (*toe-reet-sue-gee*)

edition **han** (*hahn*)

first edition **shohan** (*show-hahn*)

second edition **saihan** (*sie-hahn*);
also: **dai-nihan** (*die-nee hahn*)

hardcover **hado-kaba** (*hah-doe-kah-bah*)

paperback **pepa bakku** (*pay-pah-bahk-kuu*)

publisher **shuppan-sha** (*shupe-pahn-shah*)

read **yomimasu** (*yoe-me-mahss*)

read (past tense) **yomimashita** (*yoe-me-mahssh-tah*)

want to read **yomitai** (*yoe-me-tie*)

softcover **sofuto-kaba** (*so-fuu-toe-kah-bah*)

CHAPTER 12

Boutiques

ブティック

Butikku (*Buu-teek-kuu*)

During the last centuries of Japan's long feudal age (1192–1868) wearing apparel was prescribed by law and determined by social class and occupation. Wearing the wrong apparel was a serious transgression, and could get one imprisoned or worse.

As a result of this Shogunate government policy, the Japanese became very sensitive to clothing—a sensitivity that continues today.

After the last samurai dynasty fell in 1868 and the modernization of Japan began in the 1870s, the traditional kimono-style apparel quickly gave way to Western dress, generally except on ceremonial and formal occasions.

But the manufacture of Western-style apparel in Japan virtually ceased during the final stages of World War-II, and when the war ended in 1945 people had to make the most with what they had.

Thousands of sewing and dress-making schools sprang up all over the country, attracting hundreds of thousands of young women. The more professional of these young women went on to open dress-making shops, which stimulated the appearance of apparel boutiques.

During one ten-year period it was the dream of a large percentage of Japan's hundreds of thousands of cabaret hostesses to save up enough money to open a boutique.

By the end of the 1950s famous Japanese apparel makers like **Renown**, **Kanebo** and **Onward** were well on their way to becoming giants, and Japanese fashion designers had begun to make their presence felt abroad.

The traditional Japanese concern with apparel and appearance contributed significantly to the boutique boom that swept Japan during the 1960s and continues still today.

All of Japan's shopping areas, from the smaller street shopping strips to noted districts like the Ginza in Tokyo and Shinsaibashi in Osaka, are marked by an abundance of fashion boutiques.

Some of Tokyo's trendiest boutiques are located in the Aoyama, Harajuku and Jiyugaoka districts. Tree-lined Omotesando Boulevard, which connects the Aoyama and Harajuku districts, could be called "Boutique Boulevard." For those who are interested in trendy fashion, a trip to Omotesando is a must.

Boutique Vocabulary

accessory **akusesari** (*ah-kuu-say-sah-ree*)

angora **angora** (*ahn-go-rah*)

blouse **burausu** (*buu-rah-uu-sue*)

brassiere **buraja** (*buu-rah-jah*)

collection **korekushon** (*koe-rake-shoan*)

conservative **jimi-na** (*jee-me-nah*)

designer **dezaina** (*day-zine-ah*)

dress **wan-pisu** (*wahn-pee-sue*)

evening dress
ibuningu doresu (*ee-buu-neen-guu doe-ray-sue*)

fashion **fasshon** (*fahs-shoan*)

fit **aimasu** (*aye-mahss*)

(It) fits. **Atte imasu.** (*Aht-tayee-mahss.*)

formal wear **reifuku** (*ray-fuu-kuu*)

high heels **hai-hiru** (*hie-hee-rue*)

large **okii** (*oh-kee*)

too large **oki sugimasu** (*oh-kee sue-ghee-mahss*)

length **nagasa** (*nah-gah-sah*)

lengthen
motto nagaku shite (*moat-toe nah-gah-kuu ssh-tay*)

looks good on you **ni-aimasu** (*nee-aye-mahss*)

does not look good on you
ni-aimasen (*nee-aye-mah-sen*)

loud **hade-na** (*hah-day-nah*)

pattern **gara** (*gah-rah*); also: **moyo** (*moe-yoe*)

sew **nuu** (*nuu*)

short **mijikai** (*mejee-kie*)

shorten **motto mijikaku shite**
(*moat-toe me-jee-kah-kuu ssh-tay*)

silk **kinu** (*kee-new*)

size **saizu** (*sie-zuu*)

skirt **sukato** (*sue-kah-toe*)

sleeve **sode** (*soe-day*); also: **suribu** (*sue-ree-buu*)

long sleeve **naga-sode** (*nah-gah-soe-day*)

short sleeve **han-sode** (*han-soe-day*)

small **chiisai** (*chee-sie*)

too small **chiisa sugimasu** (*chee-sah sue-ghee-mahss*)

style **sutairu** (*sue-tie-rue*)

tight **kitsui** (*keet-sue-e*)

try on **kite miru** (*kee-tay mee-rue*)

May I try (it) on? **Kite mite mo ii desu ka?**
(*Kee-tay me-tay moe ee dess kah?*)

velvet **birodo** (*bee-roe-doe*);
also: **berubetto** (*bay-rue-bet-toe*)

CHAPTER 13

Omotesando's Latest Attraction

The latest attraction on Omotesando Blvd. is the spectacular Omotesando Hills shopping and dining complex, which is described as being the place to go for insights into the latest trends and the most up-to-date lifestyles.

Omotesando Hills brings additional refinement to tradition, authenticity, and quality by reinterpreting and revitalizing fashion, art, artisanship, and the traditional Japanese aesthetic of **wa** (*wah*) or harmony.

Designed by world-renowned architect Tadao Ando, the spectacular complex is meant to present an ideal conception of urban living. It is almost severe in its simplicity, with contrasting concrete and glass with pebble floors. The use of natural hues and organic curves blends the man-made elements of the design into the leafy surroundings. The concrete modules form a gracefully lit grid, and the exterior – at first glance somewhat stark – is designed to radiate vitality that is enhanced by trees and the essential human element—people, enjoying the space and going about their daily lives.

There are over 70 shops in Omotesando Hills, including some of the most famous brand names, such as Adore, James Coviello, Martinique Le Conte, Yves Saint Laurent, Porsche Design, Dunhill, Harry Winston and Arianne. The huge building also boasts a dozen restaurants and cafes.

STORE HOURS
Shops:11:00 a.m. - 9:00 p.m.
Restaurants:11:00 a.m. - 12:00 a.m. (Last order 11:00 p.m.)
Cafes: 8:00 a.m. - 11:00 p.m. (Last order 10:00 p.m.)
*Some store hours may vary.

Access by subway:

Omotesando Hills is served by three subway lines (the Chiyoda, Ginza and Hanzomon Lines) that stop at Omotesando Station, and is a 2-minute walk to the west from the station via Exit A2. The Chiyoda Line's next station, the Meiji-Jingumae Station, is a 3-minute walk (east) to the complex via Exit 5.

The nearest Japan Railways station to Omotesando Hills is JR Yamanote Line's Harajuku Station. It is about a 7-minute walk from the station's main Meiji-Jingu Exit to Omotesando Hills.

There are over 70 shops in Omotesando Hills, including some of the most famous brand names, such as Adore, James Coviello, Martinique Le Conte, Yves Saint Laurent, Porsche Design, Dunhill, Harry Winston and Arianne.

Dozens of famous fashion Japanese designers are also represented in boutiques along Omotesando Boulevard, including Eri Matsui, Hanae Mori, Issey Miyake, Kenzo Takada, Michiko Koshino, Kenjo Yamato, Novala Takemoto, Rei Kawakubo, Takeo Kikuchi, Yohji Yamamoto and Comme des Garcons.

American, French and Italian designers also have outlets on Omotesando as well as on the Ginza, with such branded boutiques as Gucci and Prada.

CHAPTER 14

Cosmetics Shops
化粧品店
Keshohin-ten
(*Kay-show-heen-tane*)

Japanese cosmetics shops look very much like drugstores, and are just as plentiful. Department stores also have large cosmetics sections. Both independent shops and department-store cosmetics counters carry foreign cosmetics, some of them made in Japan under licensing agreements.

The variety and quality of Japanese-made cosmetics is indisputable, and have been one of the country's most successful exports. Kanebo and Shisedo are among the brand names that are known worldwide.

Cosmetic shops and counters in Japan are invariably staffed by attractive young women who have been well-trained in the business and are familiar with both Japanese and foreign terms used in the industry, so generally there is no communication problem.

And some of the young women manning vendor counters in department stores are very aggressive about selling their wares. When I was in the main Mitsukoshi branch in Nihonbashi recently and walked up to the cosmetics counter, one of the young girls literally grabbed my hand and applied a new product to one of my fingernails that made it gleam for several weeks.

CHAPTER 15

Department Stores
デパート
Depaato (*Day-pahh-toe*)

Japan not only gave birth to the world's first department store, the country's **depato** (*day-paah-toe*) as they are known, are still today in a class by themselves. There are some 100 department store companies in Japan, with 280 branches around the country—28 of them in Tokyo.

The leading store chains in Tokyo include Isetan, Marui, Matsuya, Matsuzakaya, Mitsukoshi and Takashimaya. Leading chains in Osaka include Daimaru, Hankyu, Kintetsu and Sogo,

Besides selling everything from goldfish to golf clubs, they are also venues for art shows, musical performances, handi-craft exhibits, etc. Special customer facilities include cloak-rooms, babycare rooms, and rest areas.

Department-store rooftops often provide amusement parks for children. Their huge basement food departments alone are worth not just a visit but a field day. They specialize in all of the ingredients that go into Japanese cuisine, hundreds of ready-made-dishes to go, and a vast array of specialty foods generally not found in any other store.

Most of the food sections in the basement food centers are operated by independent vendors—dozens of them, offering everthing from beer, wine and sake, to candy and cookies.

A trip to Japan could hardly be complete without a visit to one or more of the larger department stores. They are unique, not only in the goods and services they offer, but also in their management style—which is the envy of foreign department store operators.

Japanese **depato** have traditionally offered delivery service for a nominal fee. Some also offer shipment overseas, with the cost depending on the destination and weight. All department stores accept returns, except for food and items that were on special sale at the time of purchase. Some stores do not return cash but instead issue credit coupons that must be spent in the store.

The following are some of the best-known department stores in Tokyo (several of which have branches in other cities):

Isetan (*Ee-say-tahn*)
Shinjuku Main Store

The Isetan Department store is located in Shinjuku on the west side of central Tokyo. Hours: 10 a.m. to 7 p.m. Closed on Wednesdays. There is a subway station beneath the main street adjoining the store, with direct access to the basement food department.

The Isetan is also a five-minute walk from the east entrance, **higashi-guchi** (*hee-gah-she-guu-chee*), of Japan Railway's Shinjuku Station—the busiest train station in the world.

One of Tokyo's most prestigious department stores, Isetan consists of a main building and an adjoining annex, with parking facilities on the fourth to eighth floors of Park City Isetan, a short distance away.

Shuttle-bus service is available to and from the parking building.

The main Isetan building features babies' and children's wear, women's wear, household items, dry goods, "living goods," jewelry, clocks and watches, and a large food department in the basement.

In the annex building are men's wear, sporting goods, and a museum.

Isetan has a foreign-customer service unit called the I Club, with a service counter on the seventh floor of the main building. The counter is staffed by multilingual foreign personnel trained to help foreign customers, particularly residents but visitors as well.

The I Club offers delivery service both domestically and overseas. The latter is called **kaigai hasso** (*kie-guy hahss-soe*) and is handled in the first basement, or B1.

Isetan branch stores are located in Kichijoji, Tachikawa, Matsudo, Urawa, Shizuoka, and Niigata, as well as in Singapore and Hong Kong.

Matsuya (*Mot-sue-yah*)
Ginza Branch

The main Matsuya Department Store is in the center of the Ginza district, the best-known shopping area in Japan. Two subway lines (the Ginza and Hibiya) converged a block from the store, and four other lines (the Marunouchi, Chiyoda, Yurakucho and Mita) within a two to five minute walk. Hours: 10 a.m. to 7 p.m. Closed on Thursdays.

Just north of the main Ginza intersection (Ginza Boulevard and Hibiya Street) Matsuya, was one of the first department stores in Japan to provide special shopping services for foreigners.

On the eighth floor of the store is a coffee shop and restaurants serving Japanese, Chinese, and Western food, and international telephone facilities. To call overseas, push a button and you will be connected with an operator in the country you are calling. Only credit-card and collect calls are possible.

The first basement in Matsuya, called the Marketplace, features fresh and canned foods of all kinds, wines, liquors, etc. The second basement, B2, is the Restaurant Plaza. Store directories are available at the reception desk near the front entrance.

Matsuya's Asakusa store adjoins Asakusa Station on the Ginza and Toei Asakusa subway lines.

Mitsukoshi (*Meet-sue-koe-she*)
Nihonbashi Branch

This is the mother of all department stores in the world. It is located in Nihonbashi near the north end of Ginza Boulevard. Hours: 10 a.m. to 7 p.m. Closed on Mondays. A Ginza and Hanzomon subway line station is beneath the street in front of the store, and provides access directly to the basement of the store.

The predecessor of the main Mitsukoshi department store at Nihonbashi was founded some three hundred years ago and it is widely regarded as the most prestigious department store in Japan. It even has its own subway station, Mitsukoshimae (The Front of Mitsukoshi).

Mitsukoshi
Ginza Branch

The Ginza branch of Mitsukoshi is on the corner northeast corner of Ginza Dori *(Chuo Dori)* and Harumi Dori, considered the center of the Ginza. The famous Wako Department Store, purveyor of traditional things, is on the northwest corner of the intersection.

(For those who remember the American period in Japan (1945–1952), this branch of the Mitsukoshi department store chain was operated by the United States Army as Tokyo PX (Post Exchange) No. 1. And there was a hamburger and milkshake shop in the basement of the Wako Department Store across the street.

The open-air foyer of the Ginza branch of the Mitsukoshi was the location of the first McDonald's in Japan—put there in 1970 by Japanese entrepreneur Ken Fujita over the objections of McDonald's United States who wanted it placed somewhere in a Tokyo suburb. Although nothing more than a counter with a kitchen behind it, the **tachi-gui** (*tah-chee-gwee*) or "stand-up" restaurant was wildly successful from day one.)

In addition to a delicatessen, drugstore, several restaurants, travel agency, exhibition hall, and events floor, the Ginza Mitsukoshi has an art gallery, a baby-care lounge, and a shoe-repair service. A second-floor restaurant that overlooks the intersection, long regarded as the center of downtown Tokyo, is a popular luncheon place. Store guides in English are available at the Information Counter just inside the main entrance.

Mitsukoshi has branches in Tokyo's Ikebukuro and Shinjuku districts and in several other cities in the country.

Seibu (*Say-ee-buu*)
Shibuya Branch

The Shibuya branch of the Seibu Department Store is a two-to-three minute walk from Shibuya Station, a main commuter hub in southwest Tokyo, where two subway lines and several commuter railway lines converge. Hours: 10 a.m. to 7 p.m. Closed on Thursdays. It is a member of the huge Seibu conglomerate that includes railways, marinas, hotels and resorts.

The Shibuya Seibu has all of the things that other major department stores have, plus a large and popular theater, where noh and other traditional shows are presented. Its array of restaurants is considered to be among the best in Tokyo.

The Seibu group has branch stores in the Yurakucho district of downtown Tokyo, adjoining the Ginza, and in Ikebukruo, a major transportation terminal and shopping district in northeast Tokyo.

Part of one of Japan's largest commercial combines the Seibu stores are noted for their high fashions that appeal to the young and active. The stores have a special section catering to foreign customers.

The Ikebukuro branch of the chain is by far the largest of the Tokyo branches. Its food department, combining traditional Japanese, Chinese, and Western foods, covers three huge levels.

Takashimaya (*Tah-kay-she-mah-yah*)
Nihonbashi Branch

Located near the north end of the Ginza shopping district in Nihonbashi, the Takashimaya is open from 10 a.m to 7 p.m. daily except Wednesdays. The Ginza and Tozai subway lines station is beneath the street in front of the store.

With several overseas branches and reputation for catering to a foreign clientele, Takashimaya may be the Japanese department store that is best known to foreigners.

The main Tokyo branch has designated English-speaking clerks, an overseas shipping service, and a foreign-currency exchange facility.

Fronting on Ginza Boulevard, the store adjoins the Nihonbashi subway station and is across the street from the famous Maruzen clothing store.

Takashimaya branches are located in Yokohama, Kyoto, Osaka, and other cities. The branch at Futako Tamagawa, on the Hanzomon Line in the Tokyo suburbs, is considered by many foreign residents the best store in the chain.

Daimaru (*Die-mah-rue*)
Tokyo Station Branch

The Daimaru adjoins Tokyo Station on the **Yaesu Guchi** (*Yie-sue Guu-chee*) side of the station (the east side), from which the famous "Bullet Trains" leave. Hours: 10:00 a.m. to 7:00 p.m. The store carries the usual wide range of merchandise found in Tokyo's larger stores, and includes an art gallery, a food section and a number of restaurants.

Originally housed in the Tetsudo Kaikan Building that was part of the Tokyo Station complex, the department store's new location is the north tower of twin sky towers adjoining the station on the east side. A pedestrian deck connects the two towers. (The twin towers, with their ample use of crystal glass, are among the most spectacular buildings in Japan.)

Several train lines and a subway line converging at Tokyo Station make the Daimaru one of the most accessible department store shopping locations in the city.

Matsuzakaya (*Mot-sue-zah-kah-yah*)
Ginza Branch

This is another Ginza district department store, about three blocks south of the Ginza Mitsukoshi and Matsuya stores. It is located on the east side of Ginza Boulevard near the southern end of the district, mid-way between the intersection of Ginza and Hibiya streets and the adjoining Shimbashi district.

The Matsuzakaya department store is distinguished for catering to families with children.

Tokyu (*Toe-k'yuu*)
Shibuya Main Store

Tokyu, another well-known department-store chain, has a number of stores in the Tokyo area, including two in Shibuya. The first of the Shibuya stores consists of 12 floors setting on top of Shibuya Station.

The main Shibuya store is a five-to-six minute walk via a broad throughfare southwest of Shibuya Station (next door to the famous Bunka Mura, or Cultural Village, which consists of a concert hall, a theater, two cinemas, a museum with constantly changing exhibitions, and a several shops and restaurants).

As usual the two Shibuya Tokyu stores have a large number of restaurants on their premises. The main store has a typical restaurant arcade on one of its upper floors, where shoppers and visitors have a wide choice of Japanese and foreign dishes.

Department Store Vocabulary

basement **chika** (*chee-kah*)

first basement; B-1 **chika ikkai** (*chee-kah ee-kie*)

second basement; B-2 **chika nikai** (*chee-kah nee-kie*)

children's wear **kodomo-fuku** (*koe-doe-moe-fuu-kuu*)

exhibit **tenran-kai** (*ten-rahn-kie*)

floor **kai** (*kie*)

first floor **ikkai** (*eek-kie*)

second floor **nikai** (*nee-kie*)

third floor **sankai** (*sahn-kie*)

fourth floor **yonkai** (*yoan-kie*)

fifth floor **gokai** (*go-kie*)

sixth floor **rokkai** (*roak-kie*)

seventh floor **nanakai** (*nah-nah-kie*)

What floor? **Nan kai?** (*Nahn kie?*)

food **shokuhin** (*show-kuu-heen*)

gift **okuri-mono** (*oh-kuu-ree-moe-no*)

housewares **katei yohin** (*kah-tay yoe-hin*)

kitchenware **daidokoro yohin** (*die-doe-koe-roe yoe-hin*)

ladies' wear **fujin fuku** (*fuu-jeen-fuu-kuu*)

men's wear **shinshi fuku** (*sheen-she-fuu-kuu*)

sporting goods **supotsu yohin** (*spoe-t'sue yoe-heen*)

toys **omocha** (*oh-moe-chah*)

CHAPTER 16

Discount Stores

ディスカウント・ストアー

Disukaunto sutoa

(*Dis-koun-toe sto-ah*)

Discount stores have become increasingly popular in Japan as the cost of living rises and younger generations with lower incomes are forced to shop for bargains. New discount stores appear on a regular basis. If you want to visit one, ask your tour guide or a hotel staff member if there is a discount store in the area.

One of the largest discount centers in Tokyo is Ameyayoko-cho, between Ueno and Okachimachi Stations on the Keihin and Yamanote commuter train lines—just north of the famous Akihabara electronic and electric appliance shopping district. (The area is popularly known as **Ameyoko** (*Ah-may-yoe-koe*).

In later years, Ameyoko became popular as a place to buy used Western books and magazines and candies of all kinds, especially chocolate candies, and the name Ameyoko took on the meaning of "Literary Candy Shops Alley." The area is now famous for its accessories and wearing apparel.

The area is now famous for its accessories and wearing apparel.

Bargain Shopping Vocabulary

discount **waribiki** (*wah-ree-bee-kee*)

10 percent discount **ju pasento no waribiki**
(*juu-pah-sen-toe no wah-ree-bee-kee*)

15 percent discount **jugo pasento no waribiki**
(*juu-go pah-sen-toe no wah-ree-bee-kee*)

20 percent discount **niju pasento no waribiki**
(*nee-juu-pah-sen-toe no wah-ree-bee-kee*)

30 percent discount **sanju pasento no waribiki**
(*sanjuu-pah-sen-toe no wah-ree-bee-kee*)

CHAPTER 17

Drugstores
薬屋
Kusuri-ya (*Kuu-sue-ree-yah*)

Japanese laws permit over-the-counter sales of many drugs that can be bought only with prescriptions in the United States and other countries.

Japanese doctors are also allowed to sell drugs as well as prescribe them.

It is therefore not surprising that the Japanese are heavy consumers of medicinal drugs, other health remedies, and vitamins. A recent survey counted over 85,000 drugstores in the country, with some 20,000 in the Tokyo area.

Most international hotels in Japan have drugstores on the premises, and there are drugstores in most neighborhood shopping streets and in all larger shopping areas.

Most drugstores, particularly those in hotels and other areas patronized by foreign visitors, carry a variety of imported medicines as well as foreign brands that are made in Japan under licensing agreements.

Among the foreign community in Tokyo, the American Pharmacy which dates back to the 1950s and is now located in the basement of the Marunouchi Building in front of Tokyo Station, has long been favored.

Drugstore Vocabulary

alcohol (rubbing) **shodoku-yo arukoru**
(*show-doe-kuu-yoe ah-rue-koe-rue*)

antacid **seisan-zai** (*say-e-sahn-zie*);
also **i-gusuri** (*ee-guu-suu-ree*)

antibiotic **kosei-busshitsu** (*koe-say-e-buu-sheet-sue*)

antiseptic **shodoku-zai** (*show-doe-kuu-zie*)

aspirin **asupurin** (*ahss-pee-reen*)

athlete's foot **mizu-mushi** (*mee-zuu-muu-she*)

athlete's foot medicine **mizu-mushi no kusuri**
(*mee-zuu-muu-she no kuu-sue-ree*)

bandage **hotai** (*hoe-tie*)

bandaid **banso-ko** (*bahn-so-koe*);
also: **hando eido** (*bahn-doe a-doe*)

blood **ketsueki** (*kate-sue-aa-key*); also **chi** (*chi*)

blood pressure **ketsuatsu** (*kate-sue-aht-sue*)

blood-pressure gauge
ketsuatsu-kei (*kate-sue-aht-sue-kay*)

capsule **kapuseru** (*kop-say-rue*)

clinical thermometer **taion-kei** (*tie-own-kay*)

cold **kaze** (*kah-zay*)

I have a cold. **Kaze wo hiite imasu.**
(*Kah-zay oh hee-tay e mahss.*)

constipation **benpi** (*ben-pee*)

I am constipated. **Benpi wo shite imasu.**
(*Ben-pee oh ssh-tay e-mahss.*)

cortisone **kochizon** (*koe-chee-zone*)

cotton swab **menbo** (*men-boe*)

cough drop **seki dome** (*say-kee-doe-may*)

cough syrup **seki dome shiroppu**
(*say-kee doe-may she-rope-puu*)

cut; scratch **kega** (*kay-gah*)

I cut myself.
Kega wo shimashita. (*Kay-gah oh she-mahss-tah.*)

deodorant **shoshu-zai** (*show-shuu-zie*)

diabetes **tonyo-byo** (*tone-yoe-b'yoe*)

diarrahea **geri** (*gay-ree*)

I have diarrhea.
Geri wo shite imasu. (*Gay-ree oh ssh-tay e-mahss.*)

diarrhea medicine **geridome** (*gay-ree-doe-may*)

disinfectant **shodoku yaku** (*show-doe-kuu-yah-kuu*)

dose **fukuyo ryo** (*fuu-kuu-yoe rio*)

drugstore **kusuri-ya** (*kuu-sue-ree-yah*);
also: **yakkyoku** (*yahk-k'yoe-kuu*)

ear ache **mimi ga itai** (*me-me gah ee-tie*)

I have an ear ache.
Mimi ga itai desu. (*Me-me gah ee-tie dess*)

fever **netsu** (*net-sue*)

I have a fever.
Netsu ga arimasu. (*Net-sue gah ah-ree-mahss.*)

first-aid kit **kyukyu bako** (*cue-cue bah-koe*)

gauze **gaze** (*gaah-zay*)

headache **zutsu** (*zoot-sue*)

I have a headache. **Zutsu ga shimasu.**
(*Zoot-sue gah she-mahss.*)
also: My head hurts. **Atama ga itai desu.**
(*Ah-tah-mah ga ee-tie dess.*)

indigestion **shokafuryo** (*show-kah-fuu-rio*)

insulin **inshurin** (*inn-shuu-reen*)

iodine **yodo** (*yoe-doe*)

medicine **kusuri** (*kuu-sue-ree*)

I would like to buy some medicine.
Kusuri wo kaitai desu. (*Kuu-sue-ree oh kie-tie dess.*)

mouthwash **koshudome** (*koe-shuu-doe-may*)

nail clipper **tsume-kiri** (*t'sue-may-kee-ree*)

nausea **haki-ke** (*hah-kee-kay*)

I feel nauseated.
Haki-ke ga shimasu. (*Hah-kee-kay gah she-mahss.*)

ointment; salve **nuri-gusuri** (*nuu-ree-guu-sue-ree*)

pill **jo-zai** (*joe-zie*)

prescription **shohosen** (*show-hoe-sen*)

purgative **gezai** (*gay-zie*)

razor **kamisori** (*kah-me-soe-ree*)

razor blade **kami-sori no ha** (*kah-me-soe-ree no hah*)

salve **nanko** (*nahn-koe*)

sedative **chinsei-zai** (*cheen-say-e-zie*)

sinus **biko** (*bee-koe*)

sleeping pill **suimin-yaku** (*sue-ee-meen-yah-kuu*)

stomachache **onaka ga itai** (*oh-nah-kah gah ee-tie*)

I have a stomachache.
Onaka ga itai desu. (*Oh-nah-kah gah ee-tie dess.*)

toothbrush **ha-burashi** (*hah-buu-rah-she*)

toothpaste **ha-migaki** (*hah-me-gah-kee*)

tranquilizer **torankiraiza** (*toe-rahn-kee-rie-zah*)

vaccine **wakuchin** (*wah-kuu-cheen*)

vitamin **bitamin** (*bee-tah-meen*)

CHAPTER 18

Electrical Appliance Shops
電器屋／電機屋
Denki-ya (*Den-kee-yah*)

Virtually all of the shopping areas in Japan, from the smallest neighborhood shopping streets to the huge shopping centers, have electrical appliance shops.

Some cities, particularly Tokyo and Osaka, also have large discount shopping districts that specialize in electrical appliances.

One of the largest and best-known of Japan's electrical appliance shopping districts is Akihabara in Tokyo, which is served by several commuter train and subway lines that converge at Akihabara Station. Akihabara is the second commuter train station north of Tokyo Station—so it is only about six train minutes from the center of the city.

Traditionally known as "Electric Town", Akihabara has long since morphed into the leading "electric and electronic town" in Japan. It comprised an area about half a mile long and a quarter of a mile wide, and centers on Chuo Avenue, which is a continuation of downtown Tokyo's famous Ginza thoroughfare, and runs north-south along the west side of Akihabara Station.

The district is an enormous collection (over 500) of shops and multi-storied outlets that carry electrical appliances and parts, and electronic equipment of all kinds, with the emphasis on computers and computer paraphanalia, digital cameras, etc.

Several of Japan's largest and best-known tax-free shops catering to foreign visitors had their beginnings in Akihabara. These include Laox and Yamigawa. Laox has several branches along Chuo Avenue near the station.

All of the Akihabara shops that are licensed as tax-free outlets have conspicuous signs in their front windows and/or on their storefronts, so visitors can't miss them.

These shops carry the products that visitors are most likely to want, so besides their lower prices, shoppers can limit the number of stores they have to go to find what they want.

Another advantage is that all of the tax-free shops have staff members who speak English, and know all the vocabulary associated with what they sell.

CHAPTER 19

Folk Crafts
民芸品
Mingei Hin (*Meen-gay-ee Heen*)

Japan's traditional folk and handicraft industries, many of them well over a thousand years old, continue to flourish, playing a significant role in regional economies and making a major contribution to the travel industry and general gift trade.

Most of the folk crafts made in Japan today are created by people who have been in the business for several generations, using the same tools and techniques of their ancestors, guaranteeing their artistic level.

A genuine folk craft is produced by an artist who attempts to achieve the highest possible level of quality, and identifies himself or herself with each piece produced. An artist producing a folk craft may work for months or even years on one piece.

The production of handicrafts, on the other hand, has been modernized and a single item may have gone through several hands before it reaches the marketplace. The quality of handicrafts may vary, but is generally high.

Handicrafts are referred to as **gete-mono** (*gay-tay-moe-no*), which might be translated as "common things" or "base things," while folk crafts are called **joto-mono** (*joe-toe-moe-no*), meaning "refined things" or "best things."

Over the centuries the long-term master-apprentice system in crafts raised the quality of many utilitarian products to the art level. Folk craft artists were compelled to produce master-pieces to earn the title of master.

Handicrafts as well as folk crafts became a major economic activity in the Edo period (1603–1868), during which the Tokugawa shogunate, Japan's last samurai dynasty, made its headquarters in Edo, present-day Tokyo. During this peaceful period, the lords of the country's 270 feudal clans promoted the arts and crafts to increase their fief revenues.

Among the product lines that achieved the level of fine arts during the Edo centuries were several styles of pottery, including **Bizen yaki** (*bee-zen yah-kee*) from Okayama prefecture; **Imari yaki** (*ee-mah-ree yah-kee*) from Saga prefecture; **Mashiko yaki** (*mah-she-koe yah kee*) from Tochigi prefecture; and **Shiga yaki** (*she-gah yah-kee*) from Shiga prefecture.

All of these very distinctive **yaki** are still made today and are among the most coveted of Japan's traditional handicrafts.

Other Japanese crafts that flourished during the Edo period and are still being made today include:

1) Wooden dolls called **kokeshi** (*koe-kay-she*) from Miyagi.

2) Ironware from Iwate called **Nambu tekki** (*nahm-bue take-kee*).

3) Hand-made paper from Fukui called **Echizen washi** (*eh-chee-zen wah-she*).

4) Superb lacquerware from Ishikawa known as **Wajima-nuri** (*Wah-jee-mah-nuu-ree*).

5) Fine **Nishijin-ori** (*Nee-she-jeen-oh-ree*) or silk brocade from Kyoto.

Japan's department stores not only feature folk craft sections, they also regularly sponsor exhibits and leading artists and craftsmen from all over the country.

There are also thousands of individual folk craft shops scattered throughout Japan, with the largest number found in the most famous travel destinations, including Atami, Beppu, Hakone, Ito, Kamakura, Kyoto, Nara, Nikko, Ohshima (island in Tokyo Bay), etc.

Many of the international hotels in Japan have one or more folk craft shops in their arcades.

One of the oldest and best-known folk craft shops in Tokyo is the small and unpretentious **Takumi Craft Shop**, 8–4–2 Ginza, Chuo-ku.

Tokyo's **Japan Traditional Craft Center**, in between the Aoyama 1-chome and Gaien-mae subway stations of the Ginza Line is recommended. The **Oriental Bazaar** in Harajuku on the fame Omotesando Boulevard is also re-commended. It is a short walk from Harajuku Station and an even shorter walk from the Meiji Jingumae subway station on the Chiyoda Line. Omotesando Station at the east end of this famous street where the Chiyoda and Ginza subway lines converge, is an eight-to-ten minute walk away.

In Kyoto, the **Kyoto Handicraft Center**, at Higashi Kumano Jinja, Sakyo-ku, is the place to go.

If you like Japanese paper crafts, your best bet is **Sakura Horikiri**, a two-minute walk from the east exit of Asakusabashi Station on the Toei Asakusa Line and the Sobu Line. The address is 1–25–3 Yanagibashi, Taito-ku. Established in the 1880s, the shop carries more than eight hundred patterns of paper, and has branches in Fukuoka and Sapporo.

Folk Craft Vocabulary

bamboo blinds **sudare** (*sue-dah-ray*)

calligraphy brushes **fude** (*fuu-day*)

calligraphy paper **hanshi** (*han-she*)

chest of drawers **tansu** (*tahn-sue*)

chopsticks **hashi** (*hah-she*)

chopstick rest **hashioki** (*hah-she-oh-kee*)

cloth (wrapping) **furoshiki** (*fuu-roe-she-kee*)

curtain **noren** (*no-rane*)

doll **ningyo** (*neen-g'yoe*)

dolls used for the Girls Festival (March 3)
hina ningyo (*hee-nah neen-g'yoe*)

drums **taiko** (*tie-koe*)

fans (folding) **sensu** (*sen-sue*)

fans (round) **uchiwa** (*uu-chee-wah*)

handmade patterned paper
chiyo-gami (*chee-yoe-gah me*)

hanging scrolls **kake-mono** (*kab-kay-moe-no*);
also **kak-jiku** (*kah-kee-jee-kuu*)

Japanese paper **washi** (*wah-she*)

kites **tako** (*tah-koe*)

painting brush **e-fude** (*eh-fuu-day*)

paper lanterns **chochin** (*choe-cheen*)

pottery **togei** (*toe-gay-ee*)

sake bottles **tokkuri** (*toke-kuu-ree*)

sake cups **o-choko** (*oh-cho-koe*); also:
sakazuki (*sah-kah-zuu-kee*)

umbrellas made of golden-brown oil paper
ban-gasa (*bahn gah-sah*)

wooden clogs **geta** (*gay-tah*)

wooden doll with a round head and cylindrical body
kokeshi (*koe-kay-she*)

CHAPTER 20

High-Rise Shopping

Unable to go sideways in Japan's crowded cities, the enterprising retail trade has gone and up and down in numerous high-rise buildings.

In fact, some of the most impressive shops in Japan are located in the basements, ground floors, and first few upper-level floors of modern office buildings. In Tokyo these buildings include the following:

Hibiya Chantier

Just a block north of the back entrance of Tokyo's famed Imperial Hotel, **Hibiya Chantier** is one of the more attractive high-rise shopping complexes in the city. The ground floor, second, and third floors feature jewelry, men's wear, women's wear, shoes and accessories, plus shops like the Gift Gate that sell a variety of merchandise.

There are also some two dozen restaurants, offering Italian, French, American, and Japanese food in the first and second basements. Several of the restaurants offer take-out service. Altogether there are over ninety shops and restaurants in Hibiya Chantier.

Hibiya City

Part of the Fukoku Seimei complex across the street from Hibiya Park, Hibiya City contains the usual variety of shops and restaurants in its first and second basements. The main attraction of the complex is a sunken dining and drinking plaza that is gaily decorated with lanterns and bunting during the warm days of summer and early fall.

Shinjuku NS Building

A landmark building in Tokyo's Shinjuku district, the NS building is part of the complex often referred to as New Tokyo, a forest of high-rise office buildings and international hotels (the Tokyo Hilton, Century Hyatt, Keio Plaza) that has created a new city core.

The name NS comes from the first letters of the building's joint owners, Nippon Life Insurance Company and Sumitomo Realty and Development Company.

Besides its shopping arcades, the NS building boasts some of the most spectacular architectural features in the world, including a central atrium that goes all the way to the top of the thirty-story building. The hallways on all floors open onto the huge inner space.

On the twenty-ninth floor is a skybridge that crosses over the 110-meter-deep atrium. In addition to the inside elevators there is an outside see-through elevator that gives passengers a panoramic view of Tokyo as they are whisked to the top of the building.

The first basement of the giant atrium is a large plaza used for a variety of free public events. Live shows for children are staged on weekends and holidays. There is also a large hall for miscellaneous events on the ground floor.

On one of the walls of the atrium is an open-faced Seiko clock with a hand that is some ten stories long. The hand makes one revolution every twenty-four hours. The signs of the zodiac make up the twelve-hour dial of the clock.

The 29th and 30th floors of the building house restaurants offering a wide variety of foreign cuisines. The building is worth a visit if only for sightseeing.

The NS building is about an eight-minute walk from the West Entrance, **Nishi-Guchi** (*nee-she-guu-chee*), of Shinjuku Station. When you come out of the station, walk to your left toward the Keio department store, which is part of the station complex.

In the vicinity of the store, look west across the wide street and try to spot the famous Yodobashi Camera store. The narrow street next to the camera store leads to the block where the NS building is located.

Sony Building/Ginza

A Ginza landmark since 1966, the Sony Building (on the southeast corner of Tsukiyabashi Intersection), was constructed as an information center for the Sony group of products, and still today attracts over five million visitors annually.

But it is not just Sony's electronic devices that attract such huge numbers. The building also houses a number of boutique shops, restaurants, lounges and pubs—plus broad-band service for connecting to the world.

Restaurants in the Sony Building include a branch of the famous Tenichi tempura chain, one of the Sabatini Italian restaurant group (on the 7th floor), and a Maxim de Paris Cake Shop on the 1st floor. There is a café and bar on the 8th floor.

Sunshine Building

One of the largest and tallest high-rise buildings in Asia, the Sunshine Building, located near Ikebukuro Station on the Yamanote commuter train line and the Yurakucho, and Marunouchi subway lines, is virtually a city within itself. Its hundreds of facilities include restaurants, shops, an aquarium, an observation tower, and a hotel. The building is about a ten-minute walk from Ikebukuro Station.

Northwest of central Tokyo, Ikebukuro itself is a major commercial and shopping center. If your time is limited and your hotel or home is not in the vicinity, a special trip to Ikebukuro may not be worth your while. But if you have the time and inclination, shopping in Ikebukuro can be an interesting experience.

Yurakucho Center Building

Officially listed as the Yurakucho Center building but popularly known as the Marion building, this curved high-rise stands where the old Nichigeki and Asahi Newspaper buildings used to be, between Yurakucho Station and the Ginza.

The building houses branches of the Seibu and Hankyu department store chains, plus six theaters.

Seibu Department Store has its Foreign Customer Liaison Office on the third floor of the Marion annex building to assist foreign shoppers. Staffed by foreign personnel who speak English and several other languages, the FCLO will literally do your home and office shopping for you.

Free membership in the FCLO entitles you to two-hour parking privileges at Yurakucho Seibu, puts you on the mailing list for the store's English newsletter, and provides other services.

The Hankyu department store, in the west end of the high-rise, is one of the favorites of Tokyo's moneyed class. Hankyu's counters and racks are stocked with merchandise bearing many of the world's most prestigious brand names.

The plaza area in front of the Marion is now the favored outside meeting place in the Ginza area, having replaced the Ginza and Hibiya streets intersection (four blocks away) that old-timers will remember.

A clock on the front of the Marion building chimes the hour and attracts many passersby who stand in the plaza to see the time go by.

Marunouchi Building

This new building (which in 2003 replaced the original pre-World War II building that was the highest building in Japan until several years after the war) became an instant sightseeing attraction the day it opened.

Several thousand people visited the building on its first day, and the crowds have been coming ever since. In addition to being a showplace of Japanese construction technology and interior decoration, the building's main draw is its collection of upscale restaurants and shops—in the basements and on upper floors.

Several of the restaurants offer spectacular views of the Imperial Palace Grounds and the whole west side of Tokyo—including Mt. Fuji in the distance on clear days.

There are several Shopping Zones in the building. There are a total of 45 shops and restaurants in B1 (the first basement); six shops on the first floor; 12 on the second floor; eight on the third floor; and 19 on the fourth floor.

The Marunouchi Building is on the southwest side of the plaza in front of Tokyo Station. It can be reached via an underground passageway from the station—a very useful feature during bad weather.

Tokia Building

In many ways this building, on the west side of Tokyo Station just north of the Marunouchi Building, is (at the moment!) the most outstanding of the multi-use high-rise buildings in downtown Tokyo.

Referred to as a commercial zone, the Tokia Building includes an impressive choice of restaurants and shops as well as a nightclub—the only such entertainment facility in the Marunouchi district—and a daycare center for young children.

What is equally convenient for shoppers and diners visiting the Tokia Building is that its underground plaza connects with other underground plazas and passageways in adjoining buildings, making it possible to walk underground from the Marunouchi district to the Yurakucho and Hibiya districts to the south, and then turn east (still underground) and walk all the way to the east side of the Ginza district. This is a wonderful convenience on cold and rainy days.

All of the dozen-plus large office buildings in the Marunouchi area (which extends from Tokyo Station to Yurakucho Station, about three-quarters of a mile) have both shopping and restaurant facilities. One of them (My Plaza) also has a lobby café that looks like and acts like a public rest area. Kokusai Building has a McDonald's in its restaurant arcade, as does the Shin-Tokyo Building. Another has a Starbucks Coffee Shop in its lobby.

Otemachi, the business area adjoining the Marunouchi district on the north, has more than twenty major buildings that include dining and shopping arcades.

These are just a few examples of the hundreds of high-rise and low-rise (basement) shopping and dining opportunities that are available in Tokyo. Japan's other major cities have similar numbers of highrise office, shopping and dining complexes that make the dining and shopping experience in Japan unique.

Shoppers in the Yaesu and Nihonbashi districts on the east side of Tokyo Station can take advantage of Metrolink Nihonbashi, a free bus service connecting the Yaesu, Kyobashi and Nihonbashi areas, making 12 stops altogether.

The electric powered buses take passengers to landmarks such Nihonbashi (Japan Bridge), Mitsukoshi Department Store and the Bank of Japan, which have been designated as important cultural assets, as well as to a variety of old shops that have been in business since the Edo Period (1603–1868). The exteriors of the buses are decorated with scenes from old Edo.

CHAPTER 21

Hotel Arcade Shopping

Most of Japan's top hotels have shopping arcades, general-ly on a basement level. Some of the larger arcades have thirty or more shops offering traditional Japanese products like pearls, silk, lacquerware, ceramics, damascene, screens, scrolls, wall decorations, and chests.

Many of the arcade shops are branches of some of the best-known brand name outlets in Japan. A list of shops in the Imperial Hotel arcade, for example, reads like an honor roll of top-ranked stores, including Mikimoto, Asahi, Okubo, Uyeda, and Maruyama for pearls and jewelry; Noritake for china; Kaigado for woodblock prints and paintings; Odawara Shoten for Oriental arts and curios; Sony for audio and video prod-ucts; and Odawara Express for packing and shipping. There is also a post office in the main building.

The veteran pearl dealer Matoba has a shop on the 5th floor of the Imperial Hotel Tower (A-9). It is closed on Sundays.

However, prices in hotel arcades tend to be higher than in outside shops for obvious reasons. Many hotel guests do their window-shopping in the arcades to see what is available then go elsewhere to do their buying. The arcades are very practi-cal, however, for those pressed for time.

Hotel arcade shops are normally open from 10 a.m. to 7 p.m. on weekdays and from 10 a.m. to 5 p.m. on Sundays and national holidays. Those carrying news-papers and magazines may open earlier.

Some of Japan's hotels have chosen to expand the "product lines" they offer to the public by adding spa and massage facilities—bringing them closer to the country's traditional inns with their hot baths, massages and more intimate services.

The most unusual hotel shop in Japan has to be the Tokyo branch of Paris' famous Liste Rouge, in the lobby of Conrad Tokyo, the Japan branch of this upscale hotel chain.

At first glance, the shop looks austere—almost bare. But this impression is deceptive. Unofficially known as the Cigar Club (because it includes a special display of some 150 cigar brands from Cuba), the shop features a variety of upscale products from France, Italy and Kyoto that represent the very best in French, Italian and Japanese design and craftsmanship.

The shop offers a shirt tailoring service that is unique in Japan. Patrons can order their choice of some 250 shirt styles that are made in France by master tailors and then air-shipped to the buyer in Tokyo—a process that requires three weeks. The elite Japanse clientele who patronize the elegant Conrad Tokyo do not seem to mind the wait.

Tokyo's International Arcade

Tokyo's International Arcade, beneath the elevated railway line behind the Imperial Hotel, was once the best-known and most popular tourist-oriented shopping complex in the city, with 30 shops along a single enclosed corridor (beneath elevated train lines).

The complex was made up of two sections that were separated by the street that runs along the northern side of the Imperial Hotel. As of this writing, only the smaller section on the north side remains, with a few shops, notably the enduring Hayashi Kimono, which carries **kimono**, **yukata**, **happi** coats and other things popular with foreign shoppers.

CHAPTER 22

Tax-Free Shopping

Japan has offered tax-free shopping to tourists since the 1950s. That year the government established a policy of implement a number of programs to increase tourism to Japan. One of these programs was licensing selected shops to sell certain items to tourists tax-free. The practice often meant a savings of 20 to 30 percent or more, and the system continues today.

The items chosen for eligible tax-free sales included the following:

1) Articles made of or decorated with precious stones or semiprecious stones.
2) Pearls and articles made of or decorated with pearls.
3) Articles made of precious metals, decorated with gold or platinum, or plated or covered with precious metals.
4) Articles made of coral or amber.
5) Cloisonne ware.
6) Furs.
7) Portable TV sets.
8) Stereo equipment.
9) Radios and tape recorders.
10) Cameras, movie cameras and projectors.

Other items have since been added to this original list. If there is no sign on or near the product you are interested in, ask a clerk if it is tax-free.

Some tourist shops outside the hotel arcades, including tax-free shops, will discount if you do some good-natured haggling. Some will come down 10 percent, and sometimes further, especially on items that may have been replaced by later models. Bargaining can be es-pecially worthwhile if you are shopping with several friends and join with them in asking for a group discount.

Government sources say the savings at tax-free shops amounts to 10 percent on items like radios and tape recorders, and 15 percent on cameras, movie cameras, and stereo equipment. On selected items, the savings can be as much as 30 percent.

As noted in my book *Japan Made Easy*, there are some 1,400 tax-free shops in Japan, with 170 in Okinawa and most of the rest in Tokyo, Kyoto, and Osaka.

These shops are generally located in popular shopping areas, often near hotels, and have tax-free signs conspi-cuously displayed.

Some shops in hotel arcades are also licensed to sell tax-free items. Most shops advertise in English-language tourist publications that are available free at hotels, airline offices, travel agencies, and tourist information centers.

To qualify for the tax exemption, visitors must have their passports and sign a tax-exemption certificate, which the shop provides and fills out at the time of purchase. The shopper is given a copy of the certificate to hand over to customs officials when leaving Japan.

CHAPTER 23

Tax-Free Shops in Tokyo

The most conspicuous tax-free shops in Japan are those located at Tokyo's Narita International Airport and the Osaka-Kobe-Kyoto area's Kansai International Airport—with the more convenient ones being in the boarding wings after you pass through Immigration.

The largest collection of tax-free shops in Tokyo is in Akihabara, the famous electric appliance and electronic device shopping haven. Most of these shops front on Chuo Dori or Central Avenue, the main thoroughfare of the district, have conspicuous signs calling attention to their tax-free status, and are therefore easy to spot as shoppers stroll up and down the street.

The shopping arcades of some hotels also have one or more tax-free shops.

CHAPTER 24

Tokyo's "Bargain District"

Ameya yoko-cho (*Ah-may-yah yoh-koe-choh*) in Tokyo's Ueno area became famous as a "black market" district immediately after the end of World War II in 1945. The district made its mark selling merchandise pilfered from American PXS and commissaries that served the Allied Occupation forces in the country from 1945 until 1952. **Ameya** (*Ah-may-ya*) is short for "American shops".

From the mid–1950s on the district gradually emerged as an important discount district handling imported accessories, particularly jewelry, handbags, cosmetics, belts, and wearing apparel.

The low rent of the area allowed its 300-plus stalls and shops to sell their merchandise much cheaper than outlets in other parts of Tokyo.

The latest development in the once notorious district is a high-rise building complex housing many of the shops that began as street stands.

If you are looking for bargain-priced accessories and a variety of other consumer goods from apparel to shoes, **Ameya yoko-cho** is a good place to go. It is located alongside of the elevated train tracks about halfway between Okachimachi Station and Ueno Station on the Yamanote and Keihin-Tohoku commuter train lines.

Taxi drivers and others often abbreviate the name of the district to **Ameyoko** (*Ah-may-yoh-koe*).

CHAPTER 25

Underground Shopping Centers

One distinctive feature of shopping in Japan is the large number of underground shopping centers, **chika-gai** (*chee-kah-guy*). Some of these shopping areas are so vast they are like underground cities.

Among the cities that have especially large underground centers are Sapporo on the northern island of Hokkaido, Sendai in northern Honshu, Tokyo, Nagoya, Osaka, and Kobe.

The underground centers are where ordinary Japanese do much of their casual shopping, especially when they are traveling and when the weather is bad. Thus, the centers carry a middle range of products with ordinary prices. They are of special interest to foreign tourists because of their novelty and because of their convenience and comfort, especially in winter when it can be frigid outside.

My favorite underground center in Tokyo begins on the east side of Tokyo Station, the Yaesuguchi side, where the "bullet train" platforms are located. The center is about three blocks wide in the immediate vicinity of Tokyo Station and then narrows down to two wide, parallel corridors that go all the way to the north end of the Ginza district—which is why I like it so much!

In addition to several hundred shops selling toys, apparel, stationery, handicrafts, foodstuffs, sporting goods, etc., the Yaesu center features dozens of restaurants, including a

McDonald's. The long underground mall can be used as a walk-way between Kyobashi and Tokyo stations during inclement weather.

In Osaka the Umeda underground center, which links Osaka Station with many of the office buildings in the district, is a major shopping district. The area around Nagoya Station is also crisscrossed with underground shopping streets. If you want to shop underground or just experience one of the larger complexes, ask someone to direct you to a **chika-gai**.

See Shopping in Tokyo, Shopping in Yokohama, Shopping in Nagoya, Shopping in Kyoto, etc. below.

CHAPTER 26

Shopping in Tokyo

Tokyo A Historical Overview

In the early history of Japan the site that was to become Tokyo was a small fishing and farming village at the head of a great bay that was to become known as Edo Bay. Fast-forwarding to 1457, a local clan leader ordered one of his vassals to build a castle on the spot.

Leaping ahead again, this time to 1603, Ieyasu Tokugawa who had just succeeded in becoming the paramount military power in the country, made Edo Castle his headquarters and set about enlarging and improving it. He was soon ritually confirmed by the virtually powerless emperor in Kyoto as the new shogun.

By the late 1600s Edo was the largest city in Japan, with hills, valleys, rivers and canals that made much of it look like a giant park. The Tokugawa Shogunate was to survive until 1868, during which the city grew to be larger and more attractive than most capital cities around the world.

One of the key things that the first and second Tokugawa shoguns did was to make it the law of the land that all of the country's 250-plus hereditary fief lords would build mansions in Edo and keep their families there at all times. The lords of larger fiefs maintained two or more mansions in the city all with landscaped gardens, and some with surrounding grounds that were huge in size.

All of the mansion estates were tended by staffs that included carpenters, grounds keepers, etc., and over the decades each of them grew into virtual villages of varying sizes. When the shogunate era ended in 1868 the larger mansion estates were taken over by the new government, while the smaller ones remained in the families of the former fief lords. The emperor was moved from Kyoto to Edo, which was renamed Tokyo, meaning "Eastern Capital."

As the decades passed, the areas in between all of the former "fief villages" filled in, but all of them maintained some of their former identity, which continues even today —not only in the names of the individual areas of Tokyo but also in their character.

And this is why present-day Tokyo has so many distinct areas that are essentially towns and cities within Tokyo, and why it has such diversity.

Tokyo Landmarks

Tokyo Tower
4-2-8 Shiba-Koen,
Minato-ku. Constructed in 1958, Tokyo Tower is 333 meters, and still today is one of the most conspicuous sights on the Tokyo skyline as you approach the city by air, sea or land. The tower has two observation floors that provide panoramic views of Tokyo and Mount Fuji (the latter on clear days). The first observation floor is 150 meters high; the second one is 250 meters high.

Tokyo Tower is lit by 164 floodlights that are orange in winter and incandescent white in summer. The huge ground floor area of the tower has a number of shops and restaurants, as well as the Tokyo Tower Wax Museum, the Mysterious Walking Zone and a Trick Art Gallery.

Rainbow Bridge

Tokyo Bay, Minato-ku.

This magnificent bridge spans Tokyo Bay from the Shimbashi and Shiodome areas of the city to the man-made island of Odaiba [a premier entertainment and office center] in the middle of the bay. Its changing night-time lights are reminiscent of a rainbow—thus the name.

Rainbow Bridge encompasses eight traffic lanes for cars, two railway lines, a pedestrian walkway and a number of observation platforms. Completed in 1993, the famous suspension bridge is 918 meters long. The most popular way of crossing the bridge is via the Yurikamome Monorail Line that leaves from a terminal next to JR Railways' Shimbashi Station.

Imperial Palace

Kokyo Gaien, Chiyoda-ku

The Imperial Palace, located in the center of Tokyo in what was originally the inner courtyard of Edo Castle, is the official residence of the emperor and empress of Japan. Once surrounded by five great moats, with many gated entrances, the palace grounds now have only portions of one moat (and a guard post on the eastern corner of the grounds that gives some impression of the size and glory of the original castle).

The present imperial residence is a combination of Japanese and Western architecture that reflects the cultural heritage of Japan and the role of the imperial family. On the emperor's birthday and on January 2, selected members of the public are permitted to enter the palace grounds to greet the emperor. The still heavily wooded grounds are especially visible from high-rise buildings in the city.

Shinjuku Skyscrapers

In the 1970s the skyline of Tokyo was permanently changed by the construction of high-rise buildings on the west side of Shinjuku Station (where there was solid rock below the surface that could support their weight).

In addition to the office buildings of some of Japan's leading corporations (Nomura, Sumitomo, Mitsui, Shinjuku Central, etc.), these skyscrapers included a number of international hotels and the Tokyo Metropolitan Government Building.

Most of the skyscrapers have shopping arcades on their ground floors and in their basements, and restaurants with great views of the city on their top floors.

Shiodome Skyscrapers

Once a saltwater tidelands, the Shiodome area (next to JR's Shimbashi Station at the south end of the Ginza) has been transformed into a city within a city, with huge high-rise towers that accommodate offices, hundreds of shops, cafes and restaurants, along with theaters, bookstores, spas, and hotels. There are numerous plaza-like areas within the complex that make it extraordinarily user friendly.

This spectacular complex did for downtown Tokyo what the Shinjuku high-rises did for western Tokyo. Its tall towers are among the first to be visible from the air and the sea as you approach Tokyo. Shiodome literally means "place where the tide stops."

Hibiya Park

1-6 Hibiya Koen, Chiyoda-ku.

Once the parade ground for the Imperial Japanese Army, this area was converted to Japan's first Western style park in the early 1900s. The park is across the street from the Imperial Hotel and the southeast corner of the inner moat that marks the beginning of the imperial palace grounds, and a five minute walk from the Ginza.

Hibiya Park provides a soothing respite from the crowds and traffic in this part of Tokyo. There are a number of restaurants, a flower shop and a library in the park but it is most used as a pleasant short-cut to government offices on its west side and as a place for office workers in the area to eat box lunches during the noon hour. On weekends and holidays, there are often food-cart vendors in the park.

As the heart of Japan and the city with the highest concentration of people, Tokyo is definitely the shopping capital of the country. But metropolitan Tokyo, with its twenty-three wards and numerous satellite towns and cities, is so large that many people spend all their lives there without ever stepping foot in even half of the wards, much less all of the larger shopping areas.

The size of the city, its nameless streets, and complex address system have led people to rely on the city's **ku** (*kuu*), or wards, to orient themselves and guide their movements. Although Tokyo has twenty-three wards, virtually all of the international hotels as well as most business and tourist-type hotels are located in the inner wards of the city. These are the Chuo, Chiyoda, Minato, Shibuya and Shinjuku wards.

Following are some of the major shopping districts within these wards:

Shopping for Electronics & Cameras

In Japan's amazing retail trade cameras and electronic devices are now generally sold in the same outlets—particularly by larger companies that have multiple shops—and there are two camera-electronic meccas that attract shoppers from all over the world—the Akihabara district in Tokyo and Den-Den Town in Osaka (Den-Den stands for Electric- Electronic).

Akihabara (*Ah-kee-hah-bah-rah*)
Overview of Akihabara

During most of the 1900s Akihabara was a scruffy wholesale district for electric appliances and parts of every description. In the 1980s shops in the area began adding electronic products to their stock. Now it is one of the world's largest and most impressive retail centers for electronic products and digital cameras— and is still a major electrical appliance shopping center.

There are hundreds of electronics shops of various sizes around Akihabara Station and along Chuo Dori (Chuo

Avenue), offering everything from the newest computers, cameras, televisions, mobile phones and home appliances to second-hand goods and electronic junk.

A few major stores, such as Ishimaru Denki, Sofmap and Laox operate multiple branch stores mainly along the main roads, while many smaller shops can be found in the narrow side streets.

Akihabara Landmarks

Three of the largest and most impressive landmark shopping complexes in Akihabara are the Akihabara Dai Building, the Akihabara UDX Building and the Yodobashi Akiba Building. Huge new buildings are regularly being added to the mix.

Akihabara is the largest and most popular electronics and electric appliance shopping district in Tokyo. Among its mega-stores, the giants include the Yodobashi Camera Multimedia Akiba complex, the Ishimaru Denki stores (including the 1,000 meter floor space Refino & Anhelo store that is the largest specialist retailer of audio equipment in Akihabara), Laox Company with its 12 locations, and the Yamagiwa stores.

The Yodobashi Camera Multimedia Akiba complex, with six floors and 23,000 square meters of shopping space, is one of the largest consumer electronics outlets in the country—on the scale of a major Japanese style department store. It is across the street from Akihabara Station, and has been a sight-seeing attraction since it opened.

In addition to some 600,000 items in stock, the impressive complex has 24 restaurants, a bookstore, and a golf practice range. It also has underground parking for 400 cars—a rare thing in crowded Japan. The opening of this huge shopping complex was attended by Prime Minister Junichiro Koizumi— a testament to its high profile.

Another of the larger duty-free and discount outlets in Akihabra is Takarada Electric Company. The Daiso Takarada

Akihabara banch of this chain is located on the main **shoten-gai**/*show-tane-guy* (shopping street) a short distance from Akihabara Station, and in addition to the usual cameras, computers and audio equipment, it has a ¥100 Gift Shop Floor.

Both the Takarada main store and branch across the street are licensed to sell duty-free goods to tourists with passports. The main store has staff that speak a total of 12 languages.

Another of the large duty-free outlets in Akihabara is the Akky International group of shops (three in close proximity to each other).

In addition to its duty-free and discount shops, Akihabara boasts a discount department store and the Akihabara Department Store, adjoining Akihabara Station. The store offers discounts on brand-name watches, cameras, cosmetics, men's wear, sporting goods, vitamins, imported foods, and liquor that range from 20 to 50 percent.

Note that some of the electronic products found in Akihabara are designed for use in Japan due to voltage and other technical differences and limited warranties. However, most of the shops also carry a selection of products for overseas use and offer Duty-Free shopping to foreign tourists on purchases of 10,000 yen and above. [A passport is required to qualify for duty-free purchases.]

In addition to conventional camera-electronic stores, various other animation related establishments have appeared in Akihabara in recent years, including "cosplay" (costume play) cafes, where waitresses are dressed up like anime characters, and manga kissaten ("comics cafes"), where customers can read comics, watch DVDs and surf the internet.

The main Akihabara shopping street adjoins the JR Akihabara Station on the west side, and many of its taller buildings are visible from the station platforms. There are also platform signs pointing the way to the street. As you stroll up and down the main street you can easily spot the leading camera and electronic outlets from their large storefront signs. Here is a quick-over view of the top chain shops in Akihabara:

Ishimaru Denki

This company operates 10 stores in Akihabara, including the Main Store, Number One branch and the Ekimae (Station Front) branch for electronic equipment, the Pasokon branch for PCs and the Game One and Soft One-to- Three branches for CDs, DVDs, games and anime related goods.

Sofmap

Sofmap operates as 16 shops in the Akihabara area including multiple branches, which specialize in new and used computers. The stores are numbered from 1 to 14 (Sofmap-1, Sofmap-2, etc), plus the Main Store and the Kakuta branch. Sofmap-1 has a Duty-Free floor.

Laox

The Laox company operates eight stores in Akihabara, including the Main Store, Computer branch, Duty Free Akihabara branch and Watch & Camera Branch, the Gakkikan branch for music instruments, and three Asobit City branches for hobby and game related products.

Sato Musen

Sato Musen operates five electronics shops in the Akihabara area, including the Main Store and Ekimae Number One (Station Front Number One), as well as store fronts in the Radio Kaikan Building near the Denkigai Exit of Akihabara Station.

Akky International

Akky operates three Duty Free shops in the area around Akihabara Station: Akky Main Store, Akky II and Akky III. Products on sale include a variety of electronic equipment for overseas use, including cameras, computers, televisions, DVD players and software.

Yodobashi Camera

Headquartered in Tokyo's Shinjuku Ward adjoining Shinjuku Station, this giant discount camera and electronic device chain store opened its huge Akihabara branch in September 2005. Unlike most other Akihabara shops, it is located on the east side of Akihabara Station, in the new Yodobashi Akiba Building. [Note: Yodobashi began as a camera shop, but is now one of Japan's largest electronics retailers.]

The branches of the two largest chain stores in Akihabara, Laox and Sofmap, specialize in different things. See the following lists for the specialties of the individual shops.

Laox, The Computer Kan: 1-7-6 Soto-Kanda, Chiyoda-ku. Tel 03-5256-3111. PCs, software, peripherals, and books.

Laox, The Computer MAC Kan: 1-8-8, Soto-Kanda, Chiyoda-ku. Tel 03-3251-4811. Macintosh hardware, software and related products.

Laox, ASOBIT CITY (Game): 1-13-2 Soto-Kanda, Chiyoda-ku. Tel 03-3251-3100. Computer games.

Laox, The Watch and Camera: 1-15-5 Soto-Kanda, Chiyoda-ku. Tel 03-5256-7194. PDAs and electronic books.

The Sofmap Shops

Sofmap Hon Ten (Main Store): 3-14-10 Soto-Kanda, Chiyoda-ku. Tel 03-3253-3030. Games and DVD.

Sofmap Ichi-goh Ten (No. 1 Store): 1-10-8 Soto-Kanda, Chiyoda-ku. Tel 03-3253-9190. Windows hardware and software.

Sofmap Ni-goh Ten (No. 2 Store): 3-13-7 Soto-Kanda, Chiyoda-ku. Tel 03-5256-2927. Mac hardware and software and MIDI equipment.

Sofmap Yon-goh Ten (No. 4 Store): 4-4-2 Soto-Kanda, Chiyoda-ku. Tel 03-5298-8844. Game and DVD.

Sofmap Go-goh Ten (No. 5 Store): 1-7-12 Soto-Kanda, Chiyoda-ku. Tel 03-3253-0014. used PCs.

Sofmap Kyu-goh Ten (No. 9 Store): 3-14-5 Soto-Kanda, Chiyoda-ku. Tel 03-5294-2290. used Win products.

Sofmap Juni-goh Ten (No. 12 Store): 4-5-8 Soto-Kanda, Chiyoda-ku; phone 03-3253-0828; used hardware.

Sofmap Jusan-goh Ten (No. 13 Store): 3-11-6 Soto-Kanda, Chiyoda-ku. Tel 03-3253-3663. DVD recorder, projector, audio visual equipment.

Sofmap Juyon-goh Ten (No. 14 Store): 3-15-6 Soto-Kanda, Chiyoda-ku. Tel 03-3258-3155. New games.

Duty-free Shops in Akihabara

Several of Akihabara's leading shops are licensed to sell selected electrical and electronic products manufactured for export duty-free to visitors who have passports. Here are the main ones:

Daiichi Kateidenki (DAC Akihabara F3), Akihabara Radio Building 3F, 1-15-16 Soto-Kanda, Chiyoda-ku. Tel 03-3255-5861.

Laox (Main Shop), 1-2-9 Soto-Kanda, Chiyoda-ku. Tel 03-3253-7111.

Laox (The Duty Free Building), 1-15-3 Soto-Kanda, Chiyoda-ku. Tel 03-3255-5301.

Onoden (Main Shop), 1-2-7 Soto-Kanda, Chiyoda-ku. Tel 03-3253-3911.

Takarada Musen Denki (Main Shop), 1-4-7 Soto-Kanda, Chiyoda-ku. Tel 03-3253-0101.

Takarada Musen Denki (The First Shop), 1-15-15 Soto-Kanda, Chiyoda-ku. Tel 03-3251-5408.

T-Zone (Main Shop, Musen Zone), 3-11-4 Soto-Kanda, Chiyoda-ku. Tel 03-5295-9481.

Yamagiwa Tokyo (Main shop), 1-5-10 Soto-Kanda, Chiyoda-ku. Tel 03-3253-5111.

To reach Akihabara from central Tokyo take the Keihin Tohoku or Yamanote lines to Akihabara Station or the Hibiya Subway Line to Naka Okachimachi Station. Via the above commuter trains, Akihabara is the third station after Tokyo Station (following Kanda Station).

Aoyama (*Ah-oh-yah-mah*)

Aoyama-dori, Aoyama Avenue, which goes through the Aoyama district and connects Akasaka with Shibuya, emerged in the 1970s as one of the main thoroughfares in Tokyo. A two-mile section of the street from Gaienmae Station (on the Ginza Line) to half a mile or so beyond Omotesando Station (on the Ginza, Chiyoda, and Hanzomon lines) has become a fashion boutique and restaurant corridor.

To reach the Aoyama shopping area, take the Ginza Line to Gaienmae Station, then walk toward Shibuya, or take the Ginza, Chiyoda, or Hanzomon line to Omotesando Station and walk in the direction of Aoyama 1-chome and Akasaka.

Don't miss the Comme des Garçons store. This is one of the label's two flagship stores, with the other located in Paris.

Founded by Rei Kawakubo in 1969, Comme des Garçons boasts a chain of about 200 international vendors. The label is renowned for its avant-garde fashion designs and perfumes. Open daily from 11am to 8pm.

Aqua City Odaiba

Aqua City Odaiba, on a man-made island in the middle of Tokyo Bay, should be high on your list of things to do in Tokyo. It is a recently built, very impressive commercial complex that includes 150 restaurants, bars and retails shops, 13 cinema complexes and five attractions, along with a parking area for 900 cars.

The fabulous facility is divided into three zones, the West Zone, Central Zone and Mediage. There is a 260-meter-long seaside promenade deck along the water front that connects the three zones, and provides an area for relaxing and enjoyable the extraordinary views from the island.

A large proportion of the complex is devoted to the Sony entertainment facility Mediage, a name combining elements of the words media, message and image. Cinema Mediage has a 13-screen cinema complex, offering the best in comfort and audio-visual impact.

There are two ways to get to Aqua City Odaiba: by waterbus from Hinode Pier and by an automated railway line via Rainbow Bridge from Odaiba Station (which adjoins Shimbashi Station on the east side. The waterbus takes 20 minutes; the train takes 13 minutes.

Hinode Pier is an eight-to-ten minute walk from the south exit of Hamamatsucho Station on the JR train lines (this is the station where the monorail to Haneda Airport starts).

All of the shops and restaurants are open by 11 a.m. throughout the year. Some of the shops open earlier during the summer months.

One of the most impressive of the facilities in the complex is the Ramen Kokugikan, a ramen "theme park" which opened with six ramen restaurants in January 2005, and is opening six new restaurants annual until it totals 36.

The restaurants are branches of top ramen restaurants in Tokyo, Yokohama, Hakata, Sapporo, Tokushima and Yamagata. The ramen theme park is on the 5th floor of the complex.

Shops in the complex feature fashion boutiques, a variety of other apparel shops, gift stores and cosmetic shops.

Another of the key attractions of the man-made island is a large hot springs spa resort—**Oedo Onsen Monogatari**—that features a Shogun era theme. It is the largest and most elaborate hot springs spa in Tokyo (the mineral water in the numerous baths is pumped up from 1,400 feet below Tokyo Bay).

Getting to Odaiba via Rainbow Bridge—and the views from the island—make the trip worthwhile, even if you don't shop, eat or indulge ourself in any of the services offered by the hot spring spa.

Asakusa (*Ah-sock-sah*)
Overview of Asakusa

Asakusa is one of the oldest areas in Tokyo (its great Sensoji Temple was built in the 7th century), and in some areas has maintained much of its historical appearance and charm. During most of the famous Tokugawa Shogunate era (1603-1868) it was the premiere entertainment center in Tokyo, known especially for its restaurants, drinking places, kabuki theaters and for the largest courtesan district in the country (the famous Yoshiwara).

Asakusa Landmarks

Kaminarimon (Thunder Gate)
This is the first of two large torii-style gates leading to the Sensoji Shrine. First built in the 7th century it has long since been the symbol of Asakusa.

Nakamise Shopping Street-Mall
The Nakamise shopping street stretches over approximately 250 meters from Thunder Gate toward the main grounds of Sensoji Shrine. It is lined by more than 50 shops, which offer local specialties and the usual array of tourist souvenirs.

[Nakamise is divided into seven "blocks," with from 6 to 12 shops in each block]

Shin-Nakamise Shopping Street
Shin-Nakamise, or New Nakamise Shopping Street, runs perpendicular to the Nakamise Shopping Street. It starts about midway down the original open-air mall, and runs east for some two blocks. It is a covered arcade lined by various shops and restaurants.

Kappabashi Shopping Street
Kappabashi is an almost 1-kilometer long street lined by shops catering to restaurant businesses. Items on sale include tableware, kitchen utensils and appliances, sample food made of wax and plastic, furniture, signs, lanterns and uniforms.

Rox Complex
Rox is a shopping and entertainment complex consisting of a main building (Rox) and three annex buildings (Rox-2G, Rox-3 and Rox Dome). Most of the shops in the buildings feature apparel for women and children. There is a 24-hour supermarket in the basement of the main building.

Tobu Asakusa Station & Matsuya Department Store
Asakusa's Tobu Asakusa Station is the terminal station of Tobu trains heading into the suburbs and prefectures north of Tokyo, including trains to the historically famous and dramatically picturesque mountain town of Nikko. The station building also houses a Matsuya department store that spans eight floors.

Asakusa provides visitors with a sense of what "old Tokyo" was like because it has retained some of the look and flavor the city had during the last decades of the Tokugawa shogunate (1603–1868).

Situated on the banks of the Sumida River at the northeast end of the Ginza Subway Line, Asakusa has been fortunate in that it escaped the rampant modernization that swept much of the rest of Tokyo between 1950 and 1970, and many Asakusa residents shopkeepers have deliberately chosen to maintain their traditional ways.

Perhaps best known until 1957 as the location of Tokyo's largest red-light district, the famed Yoshiwara, Asakusa was also known as the place to go for traditional Japanese food and entertainment, ranging from geisha parties to acrobatic displays by firemen on high wooden ladders.

Asakusa has also long served as the shopping center for farmers and others living in rural areas to the northeast.

The most interesting shopping area in Asakusa is the long open-air arcade known as Nakamise-dori. The entrance to Nakamise-dori, about two blocks from Asakusa Station, is marked by a huge gate called **Kaminari Mon** (*Kah-me-nah-ree Moan*), or the Thunder Gate.

Nakamise-dori owes its existence to one of Tokyo's most famous Buddhist temples, Sensoji, popularly known as the Asakusa Kannon, which was founded in the seventh century.

Nakamise-dori began as the main approach to the temple. Before long, entrepreneurs opened stalls and shops on both sides of the approach to sell souvenirs and food items to temple visitors. The tradition continues today. Present-day shops lining Nakamise-dori carry many of the foods and souvenirs that were popular during the days of the samurai.

A short walk from Nakamise in northwesterly direction there is a renovated traditional Asakusa style dining and shopping district that has become the real centerpiece of the area—where the best shops and the best restaurants are located, and which is far more of a draw for experienced travelers than Nakamise.

It is in this section of Asakusa that you will find more than a dozen shops specializing in traditional handicraft items that are still made the old way—by master craftsmen who are often the proprietors of the shops and work on-site.

These shops include the venerable **Yamazaki Chochin** at 2-9-9- Kaminarimon, Taito-Ku, famous for its colorful paper lanterns; **Bunsendo**, at 1-20-2 Asakusa, a famed traditional fan maker (it also has a branch outlet on Nakamise-Dori, the outdoor bazaar that leads to Sensoji Temple); and **Yamamoto Soroban**, at 2-35-12 Asakusa, noted for its huge stock of soroban, abacuses), the ancient "bead calculating device" that pre-dates the computer by hundreds of years.

Also: **Goudoh Hakimono**, at 2-4-15 Hanakawado, a famous traditional footwear maker whose customers include famous actors and actresses and others who dress in kimono and yukata for special occasions; and **Fujiya Tenugui**, at 2-2-15 Asakusa, a maker and seller of small cotton hand-towels that are decorated with stencil-dyed patterns that are so attractive that many people use them as wall hangings.

Kappabashi Dori

There is another noted shopping street adjoining downtown Asakusa that attracts huge numbers of people who are not looking for the usual tourist items. This unlikely tourist attraction is Kappabashi Dori (Kappabashi Avenue), Tokyo's largest restaurant wholesale district.

This famous street, also known as "Kitchen Street," is lined with shops that sell to ordinary consumers looking for bargain prices for a wide variety of kitchen-type items such as appliances, crockery, lacquerware, pottery, plastic plates, chopsticks, etc.

To reach, take the Ginza subway line to Tawaramachi Station, one station before Asakusa Station. (It is a 10-15 minute walk from the center of Asakusa.)

The Ginza and the Toei Asakusa lines go to Asakusa. Take Exit No.1 from the subway station, and when you reach street level, continue walking straight ahead. Thunder Gate is only about a 100 yards west of the station.

The Ginza (*Geen-zah*)
Overview of The Famous Ginza

From 1612 until 1800 the street now known worldwide as the Ginza was the site of the Tokugawa Shogunate's ginza or "silver mint." In the latter decades of the 1800s the street was paved, sidewalks were put in and street lamps were erected, resulting in it becoming the most famous promenade and shopping district in the city. The district soon expanded to include dozens of back alleys and side-streets that were filled with bars, clubs and shops of every description.

The mile-long Ginza (from Shimbashi on the south to Kyobashi on the north) is one of the world's premiere shopping and dining streets.

On Saturdays the main Ginza thoroughfare is closed to vehicles from 2pm to 5pm and on Sundays it is closed from noon to 5pm (to 6pm from April through September) to accommodate diners, shoppers and strollers.

Ginza Landmarks

Ginza Wako
The Ginza Wako, on the northwest corner of Chuo (Central) and Harumi avenues, was built in 1932 and its tower clock quickly became the symbol of the Ginza. The venerable store is noted for high-end fashions and jewelry—and its corner area is one of the city's most popular meeting places.

Sony Building
On the southeast corner of Harumi and Sotobori avenues, the Sony Building has show rooms that display the newest Sony products, including DVD recorders, televisions, cameras, audio sets, mobile phones, computers and Play Station products. There are also a number of retail shops, restaurants and cafes in the building.

One of the more fascinating displays in the Sony Building is a line of robotic toys that are programmed to respond to 75 different commands, can react in emotional ways to various situations, and can kick balls.

In addition to the futuristic display rooms on the first five floors of the Sony Building, the 6th floor is devoted entirely to video games that visitors can play free of charge, and not surprisingly is generally packed.

Mitsukoshi Department Store

The 12-story Ginza branch of the Mitsukoshi department store chain, on the northeast corner of the Chuo-Harumi intersection, was opened in 1930 and has since been a primary Ginza landmark (the Mitsukoshi company dates back to 1673).

Matsuya Department Store

The 11-story Ginza branch of the Matsuya department store chain offers fashion, foods, household goods, a pet shop, a travel agency and an exhibition hall. It is on the east side of Chuo Dori (also known as Ginza Avenue) just north of the Mitsukoshi store.

Matsuzakaya Department Store

The Ginza branch of this Nagoya- based department store chain offers the usual goods and services on its 10 floors, with emphasis on women's and children's wear. Its company history dates back to 1611. It is located on the east side of Ginza Avenue a short distance south of the main intersection.

Printemps

This Tokyo branch of the French chain caters to women, with fashion apparel, accessories, wines, foods and restaurants, on ten floors. It has been a Ginza landmark since 984.

The Ginza is Japan's best-known shopping and entertainment district and the centerpiece of downtown Tokyo's Chuo ward. The Ginza (which means Silver Place) takes its name from a silver mint that was established in the area in 1612, shortly after the land was reclaimed from Tokyo Bay.

The area was called Shinryogae-cho (New foreign-exchange district) until 1868, when the Tokugawa shogunate relinquished power to the emperor. Shortly thereafter, the area was renamed Ginza to commemorate what it had long been its unofficial name.

In 1880–81 the first brick buildings were erected along the streets of Ginza. When the first electric street lights were installed in 1882, people began flocking to the area to see the new technological phenomenon.

Smart shops appeared, attracting foreign residents and affluent Japanese. Horse-drawn trolley cars that went from Shimbashi to Ueno were introduced in 1882. Tokyo's first French-style cafe opened on the Ginza in 1911.

The area continued to grow in size and attractions, but it was not until the mid–1920s when Mitsukoshi, Matsuya, and Matsuzakaya department stores opened branches there that the Ginza emerged as the country's version of Fifth Avenue. The main street is now officially Chuo-dori, Central Street (or Avenue), although many people continue to call it Ginza-dori, Ginza Street. I prefer to call it Ginza Boulevard.

Ginza Street today is lined with restaurants, boutiques, specialty shops, department stores and art galleries, on what is regularly listed as the most expensive real estate in the world. The shops include virtually all of the top Japanese brand products as well as branches of top American and European retailers.

The Ginza district has been regarded as the social and shopping center of Tokyo since the late 1700s. The center of the district is the Ginza Avenue [officially Chuo Dori or Central Avenue] and Harumi Avenue intersection—which has long been regarded as the center of the city. It seems that everybody who has ever been to Tokyo goes to the famous intersection just to say they have been there!

Two subway lines intersect directly beneath the intersection, and the stations of three more lines are from one to three blocks away. JR Railways' Yurakucho Station is just four short blocks from the intersection—making the intersection one of the most convenient destinations in Tokyo, one of the most popular places to rendezvous with friends, and one of the world's great people-watching places.

Tokyo's famed **Wako** Department Store is on the northwest corner of the intersection, and the Ginza branch of the Mitsukoshi Department Store chain is on the northeast corner. Wako caters to the rich and famous—especially women—and Mitsukoshi's ready-to-eat food department in the basement is a worth a visit all by itself.

The narrow backstreets of the Ginza (especially on the west side of Ginza Dori (or Chuo Avenue) boast a collection of Japanese and foreign brand-name shops that amaze and delight well-heeled visitors from around the world. Just one of the most famous of these shops is **Sun Motoyama**, at 6-6-7 Ginza, which carries virtually every top European brand known.

Among the most interesting shops on the Ginza are those that carry gift items that the Japanese traditionally buy for special occasions, particularly the huge seibÿ (end-the-year) gift-giving season, when the shop you buy from is as important as what you buy.

These elite shops include **Bunmeido** (5-7-10 Ginza), makers of incredible delicious sponge cake (each cake is identified with a seal baked into the top); **Tagosaku** (1-22-10 Ginza), makers of a famed brand of senbei or rice crackers; **Matsuzaki Senbei** (4-3-11 Ginza), an equally famed rice cracker maker whose "sweet" binzu senbei are as famous as their salty senbei; and **Tachibana** (8-7-19 Ginza), makers and sellers of dough-sticks fried and coated with molasses.

Other famous gift-item shops on the Ginza include: **Kuya** (7-7-19), creators of the famed monaka branded wafers made of glutinous rice powder and filled with sweetened bean paste; **Akebono** (5-7-19 Ginza), makers of fukuro-gashi or bagged miniature sweet-cakes; and **Kashiwaya** (4-11-5 Ginza), creators and sellers (since the 1603-1868 Edo period) of mame-daifuku, thick cookie-like rice cakes filled with sweetened red-bean paste and sprinkled with powdered sugar and cooked whole red beans.

In addition to these high-end edible gift items, the Ginza is also noted for shops that specialize in elegant non-edible gifts such as stationary boxes (**Ito-ya**, 2-7-15 Ginza); sake flasks and cups (**Mikimoto**, 2-4-14 Ginza); fountain pens decorated with real gold and silver lacquerware designs (**Ito-ya**, 3-7-15 Ginza); beautiful furoshiki wrapping cloths (**Kunoya**, 6-9-8 Ginza); tabi socks for wearing with geta or wooden clogs and sandals (**Musashiya**, 4-10-1 Ginza); and your own chopsticks and chopstick rests for people who have everything else (**Natsuno**, 6-7-5 Ginza).

The Famous Mikimoto Pearl Company

Despite the proliferation of famous foreign and Japanese brand-name fashion boutiques on the Ginza since the mid-1900s probably the most famous shop in the district sells pearls.

The Mikimoto pearl company has been the face of Japan's pearl industry since the early years of the 20th century, when it opened its flagship shop at 4-5-5 Ginza, just north of the Ginza Avenue and Harumi Avenue intersection—and now the presence of the company on the Ginza has received a major boost with the opening of Mikimoto Ginza 2, at 2-4-12 Ginza.

This spectacular 5-story building was designed by the noted futuristic architect Toyo Ito, and is distinguished not only by the far-out shapes and sizes of its windows but also because it is pink.

The first cultured pearls were created in 1893 by Kokichi Mikimoto, and the company he founded has since grown into an international icon. There are dozens of other places in Tokyo where one can buy pearls, but the two Mikimoto Ginza shops remain the mecca for those who want the best.

The western half of the district, between Chuo-dori and the adjoining Yurakucho-Hibiya district, is also filled with art galleries, shops, restaurants, bars, and clubs.

Prices in the more prestigious Ginza shops and stores

reflect the cost of the real estate, but the area remains a magnet for both shoppers and nighttime revelers, the latter invariably some of Japan's hundreds of thousands of "expense-account aristocrats" executives of major corporations.

Hotels in or near the Ginza include the internationally renowned Imperial Hotel, the Shimbashi Dai-ichi Hotel, the Ginza Tokyu, and numerous business hotels like the Tokyo City Hotel, Holiday Inn Tokyo, and the Ginza Marunouchi Hotel.

The center of the Ginza district is on the Marunouchi, Hibiya, Ginza and Yurakucho Subway Lines, and just minutes away on foot from the Toei Mita subway line and Yurakucho Station on the Yamanote and Keihin Tohoku commuter train lines. The Yurakucho Line also has a Ginza 1-Chome Station, a short distance north of the center of the district.

Harajuku (*Hah-rah-juu-kuu*)
Harajuku/Omotesando Overview

Harajuku encompasses the area around Tokyo's Harajuku Station, one station north of Shibuya on the Yamanote Line. It is the center of Japan's most extreme teenage cultures and fashion styles, but also offers shopping for grown-ups and some historic sights.

The focal point of Harajuku's teen-oriented shops is Takeshita Dori (Takeshita Street) and its side streets, which are lined with trendy fashion boutiques, used clothing stores, crepe food stands and foreign fast food outlets.

The wide tree-lined and famous Omotesando Boulevard begins in front of Harajuku Station and goes down-slope and then upslope to the Omotesando Subway Station and the border of the Aoyama shopping and dining district.

Shops, cafes and restaurants for all ages line Omotesando, sometimes referred to as Tokyo's Champs-Elysees. Omotesando Hills, a large shopping and dining complex that opened on the north side of the boulevard in 2006, is one of the must-visit places in Tokyo.

If you want to see and experience the wilder side of Japan, Sundays and holidays are the best days to visit the Harajuku/Omotesando area because that is when it is thronged with teenagers and others who are leading the fashion and cultural trends—and Omotesando Boulevard is closed to vehicular traffic for the convenience of the public.

Harajuku is not only about teenage culture and shopping. Meiji Shrine, one of Tokyo's major shrines, is located just west of the railway tracks in the large, forested Yoyogi Park.

Harajuku/Omotesando Landmarks

Dior
The visually striking Dior building opened in 2003. Its outer layer of glass panels and inner layer of curved acrylic create the illusion that the building has been gift-wrapped in translucent paper. Open daily from 11am to 8pm.

Takeshita Dori
The symbol of Harajuku and birthplace of many of Japan's fashion trends, Takeshita Dori (Takeshita Street) is a narrow, roughly 400-meter-long street lined by shops, boutiques, cafes and fast food outlets targeting teenagers. The street begins at the small north exit of Harajuku Station and goes down-slope to Meiji Avenue.

Tod's
The clothing and accesories retailer created quite a splash when they opened this innovative building in 2004. The acutely-angled concrete supports resemble tree branches and each glass panel is unique in shape, resulting in a visually striking structure. Open daily from 11am to 8pm.

Omotesando
The 1-kilometer long, tree lined Omotesando Boulevard originally served as the main approach to Meiji Shrine to accom-

modate large official processions to the shrine as well as huge crowds of people New Year's eve. Now, numerous stores, boutiques, cafes and restaurants, including several leading fashion brand shops, line the expanse of the avenue.

Omotesando Hills

Omotesando Hills consists of six floors (three of them underground) of up-market shops, restaurants, cafes and beauty salons—with a futuristic interior design that made it famous before it opened. Several apartments are located on top of the shopping complex. Shops are open daily from 11am 9pm. The restaurants are open until midnight.

One Omotesando

Situated just a few streets away from Omotesando Hills, One Omotesando houses several luxury brands including Fendi, Celine, Conna Karan and Loewe. Large glass panels and tall vertical slits help create a stunning structure.

Snoopy Town

A wide array of Snoopy goods is sold in this store, located directly across Harajuku Station. Open daily from 11am to 8pm.

Daiso Harajuku - 100 Yen Shop

This is one of the largest 100 Yen Shops in central Tokyo, offering a wide array of goods, including clothing, kitchenware, food and stationary on multiple floors at 105 Yen per item. It is located a short distance from Harajuku Station on Takeshita Dori. Open daily from 10am to 9pm.

LaForet Harajuku

LaForet Harajuku is a trend-setting shopping complex, consisting of seven floors of fashion boutiques and shops, mainly geared towards a young, female audience. The LaForet Museum on the top floor hosts various events and exhibitions. Open daily from 11am to 8pm.

Oriental Bazaar

Tokyo's best-known souvenir outlet and especially popular among foreign residents as well as visitors, the 4-story Oriental Bazaar is made up of a number of famous vendors that carry the things most tourists are looking for—pearls, kimono, yukata, tableware, lamps, dolls, furniture and samurai related goods. The building is open from 10am to 7pm. Closed on Thursdays.

Kiddy Land

This well-known toy story has six floors toys, stuffed animals and electronic games.
Major brands including Disney, Barbie and Hello Kitty. Open daily from 10am to 9pm.

Louis Vuitton

The Louis Vuitton Omotesando store—the company's largest store—takes up five of the ten floors of the Louis Vuitton Building, which is designed as "stacks" rather than conventional floors. Open daily from 11am to 8pm.

Known during Japan's Shogunate days as one of the most prestigious locations for the residences of provincial lords (who were required to maintain their families in Edo (Tokyo), the Harajuku area was converted to a huge park after the Shogunate fell in 1868.

The park was later chosen as the site of the famous Meiji Shrine, which honors Emperor Meiji who replaced the last Shogun in 1868. (Part of it was also used as a military parade ground, and the first airplane to fly in Japan took off from the park.)

Still a quiet residential area until the 1970s, Harajuku then blossomed into one of the most diverse boutique and restaurant districts in Tokyo, all centered along broad tree-lined Omotesando Boulevard, which runs from Harajuku Station on the west to Aoyama Boulevard and the Omotesando Subway Station on the east—a distance of some 1.5 miles.

Omotesando, its main cross-street, Meiji Avenue, and their backstreets now compete with the Ginza as one of Tokyo's most fashionable districts, attracting hundreds of thousands of diners, shoppers and strollers on holidays and weekends.

Omotesando Boulevard is lined with boutiques, specialty shops, and restaurants of all kinds. Many of Japan's top fashion designers, including Hanae Mori, Issey Miyake, and Rei Kawakubo, have their headquarters and shops along Omotesando Boulevard and its extension just beyond Aoyama-dori.

Two other main shopping streets in Harajuku are Meiji-dori and Takeshita-dori. Meiji Street intersects Omotesando about two blocks down the hill from Yoyogi Park and Harajuku Station, and that intersection marks the western boundary of Harajuku.

Takeshita Street begins in front of the small north entrance of Harajuku Station, runs down the slope for about a quarter of a mile, and intersects with Meiji Street. Takeshita Street and its tiny side lanes are a mecca for young people looking for funky clothing.

One of the more unusual retail outlets in Harajuku is Sokendo, a seller of authentic Japanese swords and fittings. The main Sokendo store is in the Sokendo Building at 6-28-1 Jingumae.

The second Harajuku area Sokendo shop is in the Hanae Mori Building on Omotesando Blvd., not far from Omotesando subway station. Both shops are open seven days a week.

Harajuku Station is on the Yamanote commuter train line. The Chiyoda Subway Line's Meiji Jingumae Station is just across the street from Harajuku Station. (The station where the Emperor's private train is housed is just beyond the north end of Harajuku Station.)

Omotesando (*Oh-moe-tay-sahn-doh*)

Omotesando, noted earlier, refers to a wide but short boulevard on the west side of downtown Tokyo that now rivals the famous Ginza as a place to stroll, shop, dine and enjoy a special ambiance that is missing from the Ginza scene.

The tree-lined boulevard connects the Aoyama district (also famous for its shops) and the Harajuku district. The Omotesando Subway Station is at the east (Aoyama) end of the street and the Meiji Jingue-mae Subway Station is at the west or Harajuku end.

The Omotesando Subway Station serves both the Ginza and Chiyoda subway lines.

One of the jewels along Omotesando Boulevard is the Hanae Mori Building, which houses the designs of Hanae Mori, the queen of Japanese fashion, and itself is a sight to see—the glass-mirrored structure having been designed by the famous architect Kenzo Tange.

A café on the first floor of the building that overlooks the popular boulevard is noted as a place to people-watch.

One of the oldest and most conspicuous of the retail stores fronting on Omotesando is the Oriental Bazaar, a 3-floored building occupied by more than a dozen shops that together offer about everything Japan is famous for—from pearls to antique chests, kimono, garden lanterns wind screens, pottery, and more.

The subway station closest to the Oriental Bazaar is Meiji Jingu-mae on the Chiyoda Line (Exit 4). After exiting from the station, walk east down-slope, cross the broad Meiji Avenue, and go about two blocks. It is on the right (south) side of the street.

Another of the landmark shops along Harajuku's famed Omotesando Boulevard is the newly renovated Kiddyland, which dates back to the mid-1950s when it catered to American families who lived in what was then known as Washington Heights and has long since reverted back to its original name of Meiji Park.

The multi-storied Kiddyland building features toys of every size and description and a variety of other things for children, with particularly emphasis on all of the "character toys" for which Japan is famous. The shop is on the south side of the street, just east of the Omotesando and Meiji Avenue intersection, and just before you get to the Oriental Bazaar.

Another Omotesando landmark is the venerable antiques and collectibles shop Fuji-Torii, which has been in business since 1948 and caters primarily to foreign residents and visitors. On the south side of the tree-lined boulevard, the shop carries an impressive collection of folding screens, lacquerware and woodblock prints.

It is a short distance east of the Omotesando/Meiji Avenue Intersection (via Exit 4 from the Chiyoda subway line's Jingumae station).

There are a variety of other fashion and specialty shops on both sides of Omotesando, as well as cafes and restaurants. Its biggest attraction is the large number of young people who flock there on weekends and holidays to show off their far-out wearing apparel and make-up—and to stage a variety of musical and entertainment performances.

On Sundays and holidays Omotesando is closed to vehicular traffic to accommodate shoppers, strollers and diners.

Hibiya (*He-bee-yah*)

Hibiya is a small area adjoining the northeast corner of Hibiya Park and across from the southeast corner of the outer moat of the Imperial Palace.

Hibiya owes its prominence to its location. It adjoins the Ginza on the east, the famed Marunouchi business district on the north, and the popular Shimbashi entertainment, shopping and office center on the south.

Hibiya has several famous theaters, including the Takarazuka, which features spectacular all-girl productions of classics like *Gone with the Wind*. Hibiya is also the site of the

Imperial Hotel (made famous on September 1, 1923 the day after it opened in August 31, 1923 because it was one of the few buildings in central Tokyo to survive a devastating earthquake). There are shopping arcades in the Imperial Hotel and in several of the larger nearby office buildings.

The official name for the Hibiya area is **Uchisaiwaicho** (*Uu-chee-sie-wie-choe*), which is a district in Chiyoda ward, but it is called Hibiya because of the adjoining Hibiya Park.

The area is conveniently accessible by both commuter trains and subways. Tthe Yamanote or Keihin Tohoku lines stop at Yurakucho Station, which adjoins Hibiya on the north side. Four subway lines (the Chiyoda, Hibiya, Toei and Yurakucho lines) stop at Hibiya Station.

The Marunouchi Subway line's Ginza station is only a block away, and the Ginza Line's Ginza Station is some four blocks away. All of these stations are connected by underground passageways.

There are a number of shops centered on the west end of the Ginza Subway Station—where the Marunouchi Line stops. While tiny in comparison with the underground shopping mall on the east side of Tokyo Station, it is a busy place because of the hundreds of thousands of passengers who throng the underground passageways linking the five subway lines that converge in the Hibiya, Yurakucho and Ginza districts.

Ikebukuro (*Ee-kay-buu-kuu-roe*)

On the northwestern part of Tokyo's Yamanote Line, Ikebukuro is rather far removed from central Tokyo, but it is a major transportation hub and also boasts one of the city's largest shopping complexes.

The three primary shopping centers in Ikebukuro are the Seibu and Tobu department stores, which are combined with Ikebukuro Station, and the spectacular Sunshine building, about a ten-minute walk from the station. The area between the Sunshine building and Ikebukuro Station is filled with boutiques, specialty shops, restaurants, bars, and clubs.

The Sunshine Building, one of the highest buildings in Asia and conspicuous on the Tokyo skyline, is a virtually city within itself, with dozens of shops and restaurants and a hotel.

The Yamanote, Marunouchi, and Yurakucho subway lines stop at Ikebukuro, as does Tokyo's famous **Yamate** (*Yah-mah-tay*) commuter Loop Line train line—also known as the **Yamanote** (*Yah-mah-no-tay*) line.

Other computer lines serving regions northwest of Tokyo originate at Ikebukuro Station, which altogether serves over one million commuters daily.

In September Ikebukuro stages the Fukuro Festival, one of the larger and more colorful events in Tokyo. **Fukuro** (*fuu-kuu-roe*) means "bag."

Kanda (*Kahn-dah*)

In the early days of the Tokugawa shogunate (1603–1868), the Kanda section of Tokyo's central Chiyoda ward was the heart of the city's commercial activities. For the past hundred years or so it has been better known for its universities, publishing companies, and bookstores.

The main Kanda thoroughfare runs past Kanda Station (on the Chuo, Keihin Tohoku, Yamanote, and Ginza lines) through the heart of the district to Kudan, where the famed Yasukuni Shrine is located.

Today Kanda is the book mecca of Japan. There are literally hundreds of bookstores in the district, some carrying a wide selection of books and others specializing in comic books, medical books, architectural books, rare books, books from China, books from the Soviet Union, etc.

Bookstores that carry large selections of books in English include:

Sanseido at 1–1 Kanda, Jimbocho.
Kitazawa at 2–5–3 Kanda, Jimbocho.

Nihonbashi (*Nee-hone-bah-she*)

Now primarily known as a financial and business district, **Nihonbashi** (*Nee-hone-bah-she*), or "Japan Bridge", gained fame during the early days of the Tokugawa shogunate as the spot from which distances to other parts of the country were measured.

As it became customary to officially begin trips from Edo (Tokyo) at this bridge, the area was the scene of a great deal of hustling and bustling, picturesquely depicted on woodblock prints of the time.

Nihonbashi attracted shopkeepers and wholesalers and soon became a thriving commercial center and the founding site of two of Japan's premiere department stores, Mitsukoshi and Takashimaya.

The Ginza and Tozai subway lines converge at Nihonbashi Station, and the Hanzomon subway line's Mitsukoshiemae Station adjoins the famous Mitsukoshi Department Store.

Pokemon Center (*Pokemon Character Goods*)

Pokemon Center offers a monster selection of Pokemon goods. You may have to line up with the kids to get in. It's a five-minute walk from the east side of Tokyo Station, and a three-minute walk from the B3 Exit of the Nihonbashi Subway.

Roppongi
Roppongi Area Overview

Tokyo's Roppongi district became famous as an entertainment and dining area in the 1960s, but it did not really come into its own as an upscale office, dining and shopping mecca until the opening of the huge Roppongi Hills complex in 2003—a city within a city that features residential, recreational and office space, an art museum, a cinema complex, hotel, various shops, restaurants and cafes.

Roppongi Landmarks

Roppongi Hills
In the center of Roppongi Hills stands the Mori Tower, a 54-storey skyscraper named after the company and company president that built it. The first six floors of the Mori Tower are occupied by shops and restaurants, while the top six floors house the Mori Art Center, including the Mori Art Museum, and the Tokyo Sky Deck with spectacular views of the city. Offices fill the 43 floors in between.

Adjacent to the Mori Tower stand a few more buildings filled mostly with shops and restaurants, as well as the luxury hotel Grand Hyatt Tokyo, a Virgin Cinemas complex and the Mori Garden, a modern version of a traditional Japanese landscape garden. Just next to the garden are the new headquarters of TV Asahi, one of Japan's nationwide television stations.

Roppongi Keyakizaka Street, behind the Mori Tower, is lined with cafes and luxury brand shops such as Louis Vuitton. Across the street there are four residential high-rise buildings.

Tokyo Mid-Town
The latest landmark to distinguish the Roppongi area is another Mori Company development known as Tokyo Mid-Town, an even more spectacular complex of office buildings, residential areas, shops and restaurants than Roppongi Hills—set in a large landscaped and tree-filled park that was once the headquarters of Japan's Defense Agency. Tokyo Mid-Town opened in February 2007.

Previously known as one of the top bar, nightclub and restaurant districts in Tokyo, Roppongi has blossomed into an upscale shopping destination as well, thanks to the addition of the huge Roppongi Hills complex (on Roppongi Avenue some four blocks west of the main Roppongi Intersection), and the newer and even more impressive Tokyo Midtown on the site once occupied by Japan's Defense Agency.

In addition to dozens of high-end cafes and restaurants, the Roppongi Hills complex includes dozens of brand-name boutique shops and specialty stores.

Tokyo Midtown is distinguished by office buildings, residential towers, and a large variety of restaurants and shops in a huge park setting that is a first for Tokyo. It is located on Gaien Higashi Dori (East Gaien Avenue) a short distance northwest of Roppongi Intersection (in the direction of Aoyama 1-chome).

Shibuya (*She-buu-yah*)
Shibuya Station Area Overview

Shibuya Station is a major terminus for commuter train and subway lines on Tokyo's southwest side. The area boasts a number of landmark places that are part of the overall Shibuya shopping (and dining) scene, and make the surrounding district one of the most popular places in Tokyo. The leading Shibuya landmarks include:

Shibuya Landmarks

Tokyu Department Stores
There are two Tokyu department stores in Shibuya. The first one "sets on top" of Shibuya Station, which takes up the first two floors of the 12-story building. The main Tokyu store (with 10 floors) is a 5-8-minute walk northwest of the station. The main store is open daily from 11am to 7 or 8pm, depending on the floor. The "restaurant floor" is open until 10:30pm. The Shibuya Station store is open daily from 10am to 7 or 8pm depending on the floor. Restaurants in the building are open until 10:30pm.

Bunkamura (Cultural Village)

Located behind Shibuya's main Tokyu Department Store, Bunkamura, or Cultural Village,) includes a concert hall, a theater, two cinemas, a museum with constantly changing exhibitions, and several shops and restaurants.

Center Gai

The birthplace of many of Japan's fashion trends, Center Gai is a busy pedestrian zone lined by stores, boutiques, game centers, night clubs and restaurants, and directly accessible from the Shibuya Station Plaza.

Koen Dori (Park Avenue)

Koen Dori, or Park Avenue, is a popular shopping street leading from the Marui Department Store to Yoyogi Park. It was named after Parco department store (parco is Italian for park) and the fact that the street leads to Yoyogi Park.

Spain Slope

Spain Slope (Supein Zaka) is a narrow, approximately 100-meter-long pedestrian street with stairs leading up the slope to the Parco Department Store. It is lined with boutiques, cafes and restaurants, and was nicknamed Supein Zaka or Spanish Slope because it resembles a Spanish street scene.

Shibuya 109

Shibuya 109 is a trend setting fashion complex for young women, with more than 100 boutiques on ten floors—and in Japanese is pronounced Shibuya ichi maru kyu (Shibuya ee-chee mah-rue kyu) or Shibuya 109. The shops are open daily from 10am to 9pm, and the restaurants from 11am to 10:30pm.

Shibuya Mark City

Shibuya Mark City is a small city within the city, located just next to JR Shibuya Station. It consists of a wide range of stores and restaurants, the Shibuya Excel Hotel Tokyu, office space, a bus terminal and the terminal station of the Keio Inokashira Line

The shops open daily from 10am to 9pm. The restaurants open daily from 11am to 11pm.

Tokyu Hands

Calling itself the "Creative Life Store," Tokyu Hands is a fascinating 8-story do-it-yourself "home depot" type of store with virtually everything one might need or use in or around a house. It is open from 10am to 8:30pm, and closed on some Wednesdays.

Seibu Department Store

The Shibuya branch of the Seibu department store chain consists of nine floors, primarily featuring fashion goods and tenant fashion boutiques. There are restaurants on the top and bottom floors. Open daily from 10am to 8pm on the first three weekdays and to 9pm Thursdays, Fridays and Saturdays).

The Loft

The Shibuya branch of the giant Seibu company's Loft chain is similar to Tokyu Hands. It offers a large array of products related to interior, hobby, crafts and gifts, but with a slightly less strong emphasis on do-it-yourself. The Loft Shibuya branch has seven floors. Open daily from 10am to 9pm (until 8pmn Sundays and public holidays).

Parco (Fashion Square)

Parco is a shopping complex with an emphasis on fashion. The complex consists of numerous buildings in the Shibuya area: Part 1, Part 2, Part 3, Quattro, Zero Gate and more. Open daily from 10am 9pm (from 11am in case of some annex buildings). Restaurants in the building are open from11am to midnight.

Among Tokyo's more affiuent younger generation, Shibuya ranks among the city's top areas for shopping, dining and entertaining.

The southwestern hub of central Tokyo's huge commuter system, where several train, subway, and bus lines converge, Shibuya has one of the country's largest concentrations of department stores, specialty stores, boutiques, restaurants, theaters, and bars.

Besides its huge collection of Japanese and foreign restaurants, including all the famous fast-food chains, Shibuya lures young people with its fashion boutiques and the "fashion city" made up of three Parco department stores: Parco, Parco Part 2, and Parco Part 3.

Just a short walk from Shibuya Station, the three Parco stores are strung out along a rather steep slope that rises to the southwestern end of Yoyogi Park.

Shibuya has its on distinct character, but it is representative of more than several dozen shopping centers in Tokyo that have built up around primary transportation terminals. Here is an additional list of the shopping places in Shibuya as an example:

Shibuya 109—Shibuya 109 is a trend setting fashion complex for young women with more than one hundred boutiques on ten floors.

From the 1970s on Shibuya 109 became an icon of social change in Japan as a result of the teenage girls staffing its boutique shops wearing platform boots, miniskirts, copious amounts of makeup, coloring their hair (usually blond), wearing designer accessories and artificial suntans. The subculture phenomenon these girls generated came to be known as "kogals," which is short for kotogakko girls, or "high school girls."

Today, on weekends and holidays, hundreds to thousands of kogals (and "gal-o!") congregate around the Harajuku end of Omotesando (which is about a mile from downtown Shibuya), and are a major resident, tourist and news media attraction.

Shibuya Mark City—Shibuya Mark City is a small city within the city, located next to Shibuya Station.

Center Gai—The birthplace of many Japanese fashion trends, Center Gai is a bustling pedestrian zone

lined by stores, boutiques, game centers, night clubs
and restaurants.

Koen Dori—Koen Dori, lit. "Park Street" is a popular
shopping street leading from Shibuya's Marui department store to Yoyogi Park.

Spain Slope—Spain Slope (*Supein Zaka*) is a narrow,
approximately 100 meter long pedestrian street with
stairs leading up the slope to the Parco department store.

Tokyu Hands—Although Tokyu Hands is chiefly
known for its do-it-yourself supplies, the store carries an
amazing line of products, from travel gear to hobby supplies and Japanese folk crafts. All department stores in
Japan are generally crowded on weekends but Tokyu
Hands is particularly busy. You should go on a weekday
if you can. There are branches of Tokyu Hands in
Ikebukuro, Machida, and other locations. The stores are
closed on the second and third Wednesdays of the
month.

Shinjuku (*Sheen-juu-kuu*)
Shinjuku Station Area Overview

Shinjuku Station boasts the busiest transportation terminal in
the country. The station serves six long-distance railway lines
and a dozen commuter railway and subway lines, and over
two million people passing through it daily.

The station area is also a major hotel, shopping, dining and
entertainment district, with numerous high-rise office buildings that have long been one of the primary landmarks of
Tokyo. The spectacular twin-towered Metropolitan Tokyo
Government Office building, along with many international
hotels and other high-rise office buildings are on the west side
of Shinjuku Station. The 45th floors of the government building

serve as public overlooks of the city (and Mt. Fuji).

The Kabukicho district on the northeast side of the station is typically described as the largest and wildest dining and drinking district in Tokyo. In addition to its hundreds of bars, pubs, clubs and shops, the Kabukicho area is also known for its love hotels and pachinko (pinball) parlors.

Shinjuku Landmarks

Odakyu Department Store

This 16-story department store is part of Shinjuku Station and the terminus for the Odakyu Railway Line. It addition to the usual department store fare it also has a large basement food department and several restaurant floors. The store opens at 10am, and the restaurants open at 11am.

Lumine

Next to and above Shinjuku Station's South Exit, the Lumine complex consists of dozens of shops and restaurants on the ground level as well as upper floors. It is divided into two large sections, Lumine-1 on the west side and Lumine-2 on the east side.

Mylord

This is a 7-story dining and shopping complex that includes "Mosaic Dori"—a narrow pedestrian street between the Keio and Odakyu department stores. The shops are open daily from 11am to 9pm; the restaurants until 10:30pm.

Takashimaya Department Store

Opened in 1996, the Shinjuku branch of Takashimaya consists of 15 floors, including a food department in the basement and three restaurant floors. A Tokyu Hands branch and multi-floor Kinokuniya book store with a large foreign language section are located in the same building complex—known as the Takashimaya Times Square. The shops are open from 10am and the restaurants from 11am.

Isetan Department Store
This famous 10-story landmark department store dates back to the late 1800s, and is the flagship of the Isetan department store chain. In addition to a fascinating food floor in the basement, the Isetan also has a restaurant floor. It is open daily from 10am to8pm; the restaurants from 11am to 10pm.

Flags (Shopping Emporium)
Located next to the South Exit of Shinjuku Station, Flags is a 10-floor shopping complex featuring a Tower Records music store, an Oshman's sports goods store, a Gap clothing store and various other shops, along with cafes and an Italian restaurant. It is open daily from 11amto 10pm. (Tower Records and the restaurant are open until 11pm.)

MyCity (Fashion Center)
Sitting above Shinjuku Station's East Exit, MyCity consists of eight floors of fashion apparel, mainly for female shoppers, and has two restaurant floors. It is open daily from 10:30am to 9:30pm. The restaurants are open from 11am to 11:30pm.

Yodobashi Camera
This is the main store of one of Japan's leading discount electronics retailers, with special emphasis on camera equipment. It is located near the West Exit of Shinjuku Station, with a smaller branch located near the station's East Exit. Open daily from 9:30am to10pm.

Bic Camera
Bic Camera is another of Japan's leading discount electronics retailers. It has two branches next to Shinjuku Station, one in the Odakyu Halc Building near the station's West Exit and one on the east side of the station near the Isetan Department Store. Open daily from 10am to 9pm.

Sakuraya
This is the third of Shinjuku's three big discount electronics stores, and has nine locations around Shinjuku Station—two

on the west side and seven on the east side. All of the shops are ppen daily from 10am to 9:30pm.

Shinjuku, a large ward adjoining Chiyoda ward on the west, includes most of what is sometimes referred to as West Tokyo or New Tokyo.

Shinjuku Station, on the Yamanote Line that loops central Tokyo, is a major transportation hub serving west Tokyo, the adjoining satellite cities, and the prefectures beyond.

The station is virtually a city within itself—in fact it goes by the name of "My City Shinjuku". The complex includes hundreds of shops and restaurants and a number of large department stores. Some two million people pass through station daily, making it the busiest transportation terminal in the world.

Visitors have been known to get lost in the maze of subterranean and ground-level shops and restaurants, and wander around for more than a hour trying to find an exit.

Japan's first large collection of high-rise office buildings and several international hotels, including the Century Hyatt, Hilton Tokyo, and Keio Plaza, are from a five-to-ten minute walk west from Shinjuku Station. Two Toei Edo subway stations (at Tochomae and Shinjuku Nishiguchi) also provide access to the area.

Tokyo's most notorious entertainment and restaurant district, **Kabuki-cho** (*Kah-buu-kee-choe*), is some three blocks from the east side of Shinjuku Station. (Despite being notorious for its criminal and gang elements, these elements do not prey directly on the thousands of shoppers, diners and revelers who visit the area daily and nightly, for they are what make it so successful.)

Shinjuku's main shopping street, Shinjuku-dori, passes in front of the east entrance of Shinjuku Station. When you exit the station, turn right and go east on Shinjuku Street to reach the area's two biggest department stores, Isetan and Mitsukoshi.

Two of Japan's best-known discount camera chain shops,

Sakura Ya and Yodobashi, are located next to the station plaza on Shinjuku Street.

Yodobashi Cameras is one of the largest and best-known discount camera chains in Japan. But it sells a lot more than cameras and camera equipment, including virtually all of the popular electronic devices, from cell phones and computers to music players. The shop adjoins the plaza on the east side of Shinjuku Station.

The main outlet of the famous Kinokuniya bookstore chain is in the Takashimaya Times Square complex southeast of the Shinjuku Station complex, and is accessible via an overhead walkway from the station.

Yaesuguchi (*Yie-suu-guu-chee*)
Underground Mall

As aready noted, one of the most interesting shopping areas in Tokyo is the underground mall on the Yaesu side of Tokyo Station—the side that is the terminal for the famous "Bullet Trains," called **Shinkansen** (*sheen-kahn-sen*) in Japanese.

Accessible from the east lobby of Tokyo Station and from the plaza in front of the station, the Yaesu underground mall has over a hundred restaurants and shops, selling everything from toys and jewelry to regional food delicacies.

At its beginning, the mall is several blocks wide, with "streets" and street names. It then narrows down to a wide shop-and-restaurant-lined passageway with a center island, and extends for some two-thirds of a mile eastward to the Kyobashi section of the Ginza district—meaning you can walk underground from Tokyo Station to Ginza Street, and exit not far from the famous Takashimaya Department Store.

Shops in the mall range from fashion and sporting goods stores to office supplies, regional gifts and food items. (Among the restaurants in the mall: a McDonald's.)

There is also a branch of Daimaru department store on the Yaesu side of Tokyo Station (that will be in a spectacular new sky tower building by the time this book is out). Like virtually all department stores in Japan, it carries a selection of Japanese, Chinese and Western foods.

Yurakucho (*Yuu-rah-kuu-choh*)

Yurakucho is a small area in the immediate vicinity of Yurakucho Station in downtown Tokyo. It is surrounded by Marunouchi on the north, the Ginza on the east, the Hibiya area on the south, and the Imperial Palace grounds on the west.

The shopping attractions in Yurakucho proper are Bic Camera (which occupies the building that originally housed the Sogo Department Store) adjoining the station on the northwest side; the Seibu and Hankyu department stores in the Marion building on the southeast side of the station, and the long, curving Sukiyabashi Shopping Center, built in what was originally a deep canal bed, just beyond the Marion building.

In addition to dozens of shops, the Sukiyabashi Center has several dozen restaurants, most of them in the first basement of the north end of the complex. These include a typical collection of traditional and contemporary Japanese restaurants, from grilled fish to noodles and rice dishes with a variety of toppings.

The curving shopping and dining center continues for some two blocks on the southside of Harumi Street—ending about half a block east of the Imperial Hotel Tower and the famed Takarazuka Theater. The long curving center is a kind of dividing line between the Yurakucho and Hibiya districts and the Ginza.

Bic Camera is the most distinctive and interesting of the shopping centers in Yurakucho. It is an electronic device superstore, carrying far more than cameras and camera equipment. Computers, software, TV sets, stereo equipment, communications devices, and more just begin to suggest the things you find there.

Tokyo's Yebisu Garden Place

Developed on the site of a former brewery, this impressive shopping and dining complex includes a variety of restaurants, a Mitsukoshi Department Store, dozens of boutiques, movie theaters, a beer museum, and the Metropolitan Museum of Photography. It has a "chateau" housing the French restaurant Taillevent-Robuchon.

The complex, a favorite rendezvous for dating couples, for people out shopping and dining, is about five minutes from JR Yebisu Station via the Yebisu Skywalk, an elevated moving walkway.

Restaurants on the upper floors of the main tower building provide eagle-eye views of Tokyo—and on clear days, magnificent Mt. Fuji some 70 miles (112 km) away.

It is one of many "experience places" in Tokyo that attract sightseers because of its design and overall ambiance. (Another such place being the Marunouchi district adjoining Tokyo Station on the west and southwest sides—the basements and first floors of its impressive collection of upscale buildings include cafes, restaurants and a wide variety of shops. On good weather days, some of the cafes and restaurants expand into the building patios.)

Spa La Qua

Another shopping (and dining and spa) experience in Tokyo is the Spa La Qua complex in Suidobashi. It has a "built-in" roller coaster and a ferris wheel (the roller coaster goes "through" the spoke-less ferris wheel)— making it a fun place for adults and kids alike.

All-Japan Products Store

For visitors who are not going to travel outside of Tokyo but would like to see a wide range of specialty products from all over Japan the All-Japan Products Association operates a store called **Mura Kara Machi Kara** (*Muu-rah Kah-rah Mah-chee Kah-rah*), which can be translated as "From Village & Town Store," in the Kotsu Kaikan Building just across the street from the north end of Yurakucho Station in downtown Tokyo. This is the building that houses the Japan National Tourist Organization offices (on the 10th floor), with a Tourist Information Center (TIC) on the same floor.

The **Mura Kara Machi Kara** shop is located on the first floor on the north side of the building, with entrances from that side of the building as well as from the interior of the building on the left side of the second corridor. Both of these entrances are inconspicuous, but there is an English sign pasted on the door that reads: This store carries specialty products created by small and medium-scale regional companies from all over Japan.

CHAPTER 27

Shopping in Yokohama

Yokohama, 30 minutes by train southwest of Tokyo, has long been one of Japan's most famous port cities. In recent decades it has taken something of a back seat to Tokyo but many foreign residents and visitors as well continue to like Yokohama better than the capital.

The pace is definitely slower, and Yokohama has more of a stately, cosmopolitan air, reflecting the 1880s when it was Japan's leading international city. Many Tokyo residents regularly go to Yokohama to shop and eat in its flourishing Chinatown.

Yokohama has three well-known shopping areas: Isezakicho, Motomachi and Chinatown. Of the three, Isezakicho boasts the city's largest collection of department stores, boutiques, theaters, bars, etc.

One popular shopping spot in Yokohama is the Silk Center in the International Trade and Tourism building (*Kokusai Boeki Kanko Kaikan*), located in Yamashita-cho near the port area. In addition to a museum devoted to silk, the center includes a shopping arcade that specializes in silk products.

Yokohama Minato Mirai 21

This "city of the future" complex in Yokohama is one of the most spectacular shopping, entertainment, dining, office and hotel facilties in the country.

Minato Mirai (*Me-nah-toe Me-rye*) literally means "Harbor of the Future." It is a futuristic, new city area in Central Yokohama consisting of office and residential space, hotels, shopping centers, restaurants, convention centers and public parks.

The Landmark Tower (296 meters) is one of Japan's tallest buildings and the symbol of Minato Mirai 21. It was completed in 1993 and houses many offices, a hotel, restaurants, a shopping center and other community space.

Visitors can access the building's observatory deck, the "Sky Garden" on the 69th floor by means of the world's fastest elevator (750 meters per minute). Under good weather conditions, Mount Fuji can be seen from the observatory deck.

Pacifico Yokohama is one of the world's largest convention centers, located a few hundred meters from the Landmark Tower. It includes the round-shaped Yokohama Grand Intercontinental Hotel, which, together with the nearby Ferris Wheel (of the Yokohama Cosmo World amusement park), is one of Yokohama's most extraordinary sights.

The train station nearest to the huge complex is Minato Mirai Station on the Minato Mirai Line, two stations from Yokohama Station. (Trains on this line go all the way to Shibuya Station in southwest Tokyo.)

Minato Mirai is just a short walk from Sakuragicho Station on the JR Keihin-Tohoku Line (Negishi Line) and Yokohama Subway Line.

If you go to just two places in Yokohama, I recommend Minato Mirai and China Town, which comprised the largest collection of Chinese restaurants and shops selling Chinese merchandise in the country.

The old "in" shopping street in Yokohama is the main thoroughfare of the Muromachi district.

Bay Quarter Yokohama

Another extraordinary choice for both dining and shopping in Yokohama is the new (August, 2006) Bay Quarter Yokohama shopping center that looks and feels like a resort spa. Situated near JR East Yokohama Station and overlooking Minato Mirai and Yokohama Bay, the multi-level complex has a series of curved promenades that give the impression you are on a luxury cruise ship.

The spectacular new addition to the Yokohama skyline has 75 shops, restaurants and service facilities that include a salt-water pool, a yoga studio, and a massage parlor whose rooms are charged with an extra amount of oxygen to help rejuvenate its patrons.

CHAPTER 28

Shopping in Nagoya

Nagoya is said to have been the only city in Japan that took advantage of World War II destruction to redesign and reline its streets, resulting in a grid-pattern of wide avenues and boulevards that make it unique in Japan.

Another feature of Nagoya that sets it apart is its number of underground shopping malls. Nagoya's central train station sets on top of a massive mall that goes off in all directions.

The Sakae Underground Shopping Center between Nishiki Avenue and Hirokoji Avenue adjoining Sakae Subway Station is one of the largest underground shopping malls in Japan.

Nagoya, mid-way between Tokyo and Kyoto on Japan's famous

Bullet Train line, is sometimes called the "White Town" because of the many white buildings lining the downtown streets, and the absence of the hustle and bustle common to big cities.

The Tokaido Shinkansen "Bullet Train," other JR and privately owned railroad lines, and two city subway lines converge at Nagoya Station, making it a major terminal.

Below the station an underground shopping mall stretches outward like the meshes of a net, with connections to all the transportation lines and major buildings in the area. Each underground corridor has its own name, such as **Yunimoru** (*Uni Mall*) or **San Rodo** (*Sun Road*). The passageways link up to form a seemingly endless maze, so it is no wonder that out-of-towners invariably get lost on their first trip in Nagoya's underground world.

The oldest corridor, Sun Road, opened in March 1957 as Japan's first underground shopping center. At the time, car ownership was on the rise, and the area around the station was the scene of an increasing number of accidents. Meanwhile, plans had been put forth for the construction of a city subway system.

The concept of "cars above and people below" took hold, and local businesses ultimately decided to build an underground complex that would extend from the subway entrance to Nagoya Station. The success of the venture attracted nationwide attention and a constant stream of observers.

As business boomed, a string of extensions were made to the complex. Today the combined store space covers 27,000 square meters, and the total length of the passageways comes to seven kilometers. The number of shops is roughly 300, though according to Nagoya Underground, Inc., the total rises to 700 or 800 if the basement shops and restaurants in buildings and department stores are included.

Clothing, food, books, and compact discs are just some of things you can buy in this amazing underground city.

Each day over 200,000 people pass through the corridors of the mall, and many of them stop to shop, and dozens of thousands patronize the underground restaurants, especially when the weather is bad.

In the fall of 1999 construction was completed on the JR Central Towers—two skyscrapers designed to serve as the main Nagoya Station buildings. The first rises 245 meters with 51 stories of office space, and the second, which houses a hotel and rents space to department stores and restaurants, rises 226 meters with 53 stories.

Both towers are thriving as the city's newest landmark. They are also breathing new life into the underground maze.

Another underground shopping complex is located two stops away from Nagoya Station—a four-minute ride—in Sakae, the heart of the city. Here subway lines intersect Sakae in all four directions.

Above ground Nagoya's Central Park spreads out from Television Tower and provides the venue for festivals and a host of other events. The underground shopping center, also called Central Park, extends from north to south, offering shops targeted at young men and women.

South of Central Park there is a corridor running east to west known as **Sakae Chika** (*Sah-kie Chee-kah*), or Sakae Underground. At its center is **Kurisutaru Hiroba** (*Crystal Plaza*), a popular meeting place. Sakae's Sunshine Shopping Center boasts a giant ferris wheel.

Many of the Nagoya's above-ground business and shopping areas are located downtown, concentrated along the axes of the Higashiyama and Meijo subway lines, with Nagoya Station and Sakae forming the nucleus for the city.

JR Central Towers, the city's most conspicuous landmark and the largest building in Japan, houses a Takashimaya Department Store and the Nagoya Marriott Associa Hotel.

Numerous hotels, department stores, movie theaters, business offices and underground shopping malls also dot the area.

Two of the most famous products made or created in the Nagoya area and sold at shops in Nagoya:

Ando Cloisonne—Facing Otsu street in Sakae, opposite Matsuzakaya Department store.

Mikimoto Pearls—Facing Otsu street; between Mitsukoshi and Matsuzakaya department stores. The famous Mikimoto Pearl Farm (where cultured pearls were first created) is a short train ride from Nagoya. It is visited annually by dozens of thousands of people who go to shop as well as to tour the "underwater farming" facilities.

Nagoya's Osu Kannon Outdoor Shopping Arcade is a center of electronic equipment retailers, along with dozens of other shops. The arcade is about a 15-minute walk from Sakae Station.

CHAPTER 29

Shopping in Kyoto

Historical Profile of Kyoto

Kyoto was founded in 794 by the Imperial Court when it was decided to move the capital out of nearby Nara. The layout of the city was patterned after the capital of China—and the following Heian era (from 794-1185) ranks as Japan's first "golden age."

While Japan was ruled by shoguns from 1185 to 1868, the institution of the imperial family was maintained and Kyoto remained both the imperial capital and the cultural capital of Japan, giving rise to most of the arts and crafts for which the country has long been famous.

Over this long period most of Kyoto was destroyed several times by natural and man-made calamities, but it was always rebuilt. It is now the country's seventh largest city with a population of 1.4 million people.

A Mecca for "Cultural Shopping"

Every year several million Japanese and foreign tourists travel to Kyoto to shop for its famous arts and crafts (as well as to dine in its distinctive Kyoto-style restaurants). In addition to the inexpensive souvenir-type of things, the city remains known for arts and crafts that are still made in the traditional way by the descendants of masters that go back for centuries.

Famous Kyoto Landmarks

Central Kyoto
The Kyoto Imperial Palace: The residence of the emperors until 1868.

Nijo Castle: The residence of Tokugawa shoguns when they visited Kyoto.

Nijo Jinja: An exclusive inn for visiting feudal lords until 1868.

Toji Temple: A famous temple with the tallest pagoda in Japan.

Honganji Temple (head temple of the Jodo-Shinshu sect of Buddhism)

Eastern Kyoto
Sanjusangendo: A huge exhibit hall that contains 1001 Kannon statues.

Kyomizudera: A huge hillside temple complex famous for its large terrace that overlooks the city.

Kodaiji: The Kyoto temple that honors the great feudal leader Toyotomi Hideyoshi.

Gion: The most famous geisha district in Kyoto and in Japan.

Yasaka Shrine: An ancient shrine famous for its annual Gion Festival.

Heian Shrine: A famous shrine in the form of the former Imperial Palace.

Nanzenji: A temple with one of the most famous rock gardens in Kyoto.

Path of Philosophy: A walking trail famous for its springtime cherry blossoms.

Ginkakuji: Temple of the Silver Pavilion.

Northern Kyoto
Kinkakuji: Temple of the Golden Pavilion.

Ryoanji: A Zen temple famous for its rock garden.
Daitokuj: A large complex of Zen temples.

Western Kyoto
Katsura Villa: One of the most famous and beautiful examples of traditional Japanese architecture, formerly the residence of an imperial prince.

Kyoto Station

Antiquity and cultural treasures aside, one of the most interesting (convenient and useful) landmarks in present-day Kyoto is the new Kyoto Station complex. Completed in 1997, on the 1,200th anniversary of the founding of the city, the 15-story building complex includes a department store, hotel, theater, game center, shopping mall, government offices, dozens of name-brand restaurants and an observation deck.

In addition to all of these facilities, Kyoto Station is the city's main station served by all trains of Japan Railways, including the famous JR "Bullet Trains" (Shinkansen), Kintetsu Railways, and subway lines. A large bus terminal is located in front of the station building.

Kyoto Overview

About 350 miles (560 km) southwest of Tokyo, Kyoto was Japan's imperial capital from 794 until 1868. With a highy sophisticated market made up of members of the Royal Court, well-to-do government officials and leading businessmen, Kyoto quickly became the center of production for many of Japan's most highly prized products.

These included: brocade, ceramics, cloissone, damascene, dolls, fans, lacquerware, pottery, silk, scrolls, and screens.

Today, Kyoto is the destination of several million visitors annually, both foreigners and Japanese, who are attracted not only by the city's hundreds of historical buildings and artifacts, but by its traditional products and many festivals.

In Kyoto the main shopping areas for gifts and souvenirs are a long stretch of Kawaramachi Street, which bisects the city, and two covered shopping streets just west of this main thoroughfare. Shops specializing in antiques are concentrated on Shinmonzen Street and Teramachi Street.

Following are some of the popular items found in Kyoto shops: antiques and curios, bamboo products, china and pottery, cloissone, damascene, dolls, folk crafts, Japanese umbrellas, kimono and **happi** (*hop-pee*) coats, lacquerware, pearls, silk and stone lanterns.

Many visitors to Kyoto who have shopping for traditional Japanese handicrafts on their minds and want to save a lot of time (and money) choose to go directly to the Kyoto Handicraft Center (KHC), located just north of the famous and ancient Heian Shrine (which plays a major role in the cultural life of the city).

Shops making up the Kyoto Handicraft Center feature virtually every category of crafts that Japan is famous for—many of which originated in Kyoto centuries ago. There is also a large selection of more contemporary items that have been given a traditional touch.

Visitors can watch artists at work and take part in classes on cloisonne making, woodblock printing, doll making, incense bag making, and doll painting. All of these crafts are products of traditional Kyoto styles.

On average, each workshop lasts between forty minutes and one hour, depending on how long it takes the individual to complete the craft. Participants can take part on an individual basis without advance reservations.

The Kyoto Handicraft Center is a licensed Duty Free Shop for visitors with passports. Tour operators and some local hotels run regular shuttle buses to the Center. Its hours are 10 a.m. to 6 p.m. Closed on January 1–3.

Kyoto Silk Co., one of the KHC vendors, provides Internet-based mail-order service for kimono and other traditional items.

Kyoto's Otesuji Shopping Mall, while oriented toward residents of the city, is notable for its design and use of solar panels to provide lighting. If you have the time it is worth a visit.

As the nation's capital for nearly 1,500 years, Kyoto was the birthplace of a number of crafts and art forms that catered to the refined tastes of members of the Imperial Court and the upper classes.

Among the traditional products that Kyoto is still known for today are Nishijin textiles, Yuzen-dyed fabrics, pottery, fans, dolls, cutlery, gold-leaf work, umbrellas, paper lanterns, combs, Noh masks, cloisonné, and lacquer ware.

Kyoto may appear intimidating to newcomers but when it was planned in the 8th century the layout was patterned after that of the Chinese capital of Peking, with east-west and north-south streets at right angles to each other—and unlike virtually all other cities in Japan most of the streets in the central part of Kyoto are named.

The main east-west streets are about 500 meters apart, and are named 1st Avenue *(Ichijo)*, 2nd Avenue *(Nijo)*, 3rd Avenue *(Sanjo)*, 4th Avenue *(Shijo)*, etc. in ascending order from north to south. There a number of smaller streets and lanes in between these major thoroughfares.

Major north-south thoroughfares have names instead of numbers. The most prominent north-south street is Karasuma Dori (Karasuma Street or Avenue), which runs from Kyoto Station, on 8th Avenue, through the center of the city to the Kyoto Imperial Palace.

The largest collection of the city's bars, pubs, restaurants and shops are concentrated around the intersection of Shijo (4th Avenue) and Kawaramachi Street.

Another major shopping area is Kyomizuzaka Street in Teramachi (literally "Temple Town") on the east side of the famous Gion district. Between Sanjo (3rd Avenue) and Marutamachi, this street is lined with small shops offering gifts and souvenirs that include local crafts and paintings.

There are dozens of smaller **shotengai** (shopping streets) in Kyoto, generally in the vicinity of one of the city's major shrines, temples and other tourist attractions. Interestingly, one of the largest collections of shops and restaurants—and certainly the most convenient for visitors who arrive and depart by train—is Kyoto Station.

In fact, Kyoto Station is a dining and shopping paradise, with first-class restaurants and brand-name shops that meet the needs and tastes of the most discriminating diners and shoppers.

The following individual shops and emporiums are among the largest and best known places in Kyoto that cater specifically to visitors from abroad.

Kyoto Handicraft Center

On Marutamachi Street just north of the famous Heian Shrine, the Kyoto Handicraft Center is noted for the authenticity of its arts and crafts, made in the traditional way by local artists and craftsmen—some of whom are typically there working on site and demonstrating their arts.

The Center is a licensed duty-free outlet and money exchanger, accepts most credit cards, and provides international shipping service for customers. It is open from 10am to 6pm daily except for January 1-3. Most of the staff speak passable English.

Amita Corporation

One of the oldest and best-known purveyors to the tourist trade with shops in Tokyo and elsewhere, the Kyoto branch of Amita is located on Marutamachi just north of the Heian Shrine and next to the Kyoto Handicraft Center.

The first floor of the 5-story building features damascene and cloisonné products, with ongoing demonstrations of how they are made. Many of the items are inlaid with 24K gold and silver. The second floor offers modern gift and souvenir items, as well as sake and green tea. It also has a restaurant that serves Japanese dishes. The third floor is dedicated to more

upscale arts and crafts, including pottery, tea ceremony para-
phernalia, fans, woodblock prints, etc.

Amita is open daily from 9am to 6pm, except on New Year's
Day.

Amita Shin-Miyako Hotel Branch, B1F, Nishi-
Kujoin machi, Minami-ku, Kyoto. Tel. 671-8528

Oshido

This famous Kyoto shop has been in business for over a hundred years, and is known for its kimono and yukata, Kyoto
dolls, ceramics, silk products, traditional footwear, samurai
swords and vast collection of Japanese style accessories.
There is a Japanese restaurant on the second floor.

Oshido accepts most credit cards and its experienced staff
speak English. It is located on the south side of the approach
to Kyoto's famous Kiyomizu Temple, and is open daily from
10am to 4:30pm.

Duty Free Kyoto (Taniyama Musen)

On the 6th floor of the Taniyayam Musen's main building in
the center of Kyoto's discount electronics district, Duty Free
Kyoto carries digital cameras and videos, portable CD players,
etc., by Canon, JVC, Panasonic, Sanyo, Sony, etc., designed for
the international market. English is spoken and there are
English-language manuals for the various products. Most credit cards accepted. Duty-free shopping is available only on purchases of ¥10,001 and above (with passport).

Duty Free Kyoto is located on the west side of Teramachi
Avenue, south of Shijo (4th Avenue). It is open from 10am to
8pm.

Wafu Living Store

Wafu Living Store is in the Tozando Bldg., 2F, located on the south side of Nakadachiuri, east of Chiekoin. It is open 9am to 6pm on weekdays only. The shop prides itself on carrying everything needed to live Japanese style—from clothing and accessories to tea ceremony things, pottery, Japanese sweets, chopsticks, lamp shades, woodblock prints, hanging scrolls, fans, paper crafts and more. It also offers a world-wide shipping service and online shopping.

Kyoto Museum of Traditional Crafts
(Fureai Kan)

The gift shop in this museum carries a variety of Kyoto's famous arts and crafts, and features yuzen dyeing exhibitions as well as hands-on handicraft workshop experience for visitors.

It is on Nijo (2nd Avenue) east of Higashi-Oji in the first basement of the Miyako Messe Building. The museum and gift shop are open weekdays from 9am to 5pm.

Taiko Center

Japanese style drumming has become a big thing in entertainment circles around the world, and this shop offers live performances as well as all of the drumming equipment needed to you to do it yourself. You can also join a class and learn how to make your own drums.

The center is located at 113-4 Takatsuji Omiya-cho in Shimogyo-ku, and is open from 11am to 6pm. Closed on Sundays and in mid-August during the Obon Festival. Tel 813-8615.

Gallery Gado

This gallery sells modern woodblock prints with traditional themes. All prints are authenticated, and include postcard-sized prints. The shop is located at 27 Miyashiki-cho, Hirano, Kita-ku, on Kinukake no Michi (Hanging Silk Road) near the famous Kinkaku-Ji (Temple of the Golden Pavilion). It is open from 10am to 6pm daily.

Here is a list of well-known Kyoto shops that specialize in specific categories:

Bamboo Products

Takeihei—Over 200 kinds of bamboo; west side of Omiya, north of Gojo (5th Avenue). Tel 801-6453.

Oike—Bamboo products of all kinds are on display in this spectacular show room; west side of Aburanokoji, north of Shijo (4th Avenue). Tel 221-3211.

Maeda Heihachi Shoten—Fine bamboo blinds; west side of Teramachi, south of Shijo (4th Avenue). Tel 351-2749.

Ceramics

Roku Roku Do—An exquisite selection of ceramic art (Kyoto pottery and modern works), sold in a beautiful traditional atmosphere that dates from 1874. It is located near (and on the street leading to) the famous Kiyomizu temple in Higashiyama.
Call for hours. 075-525-0066.

Chochin (Paper Lanterns)

Miura Shomei—Hand-crafted paper lanterns; north side of Shijo (4th Avenye), a little west of Higashioji. Tel 561-2816.

Chopsticks

Ichihara Heibei Shoten—Especially beautiful and sophisticated chopsticks for every occasion.It is on Sakaimachi, south of Shijo (4th Avenue). Open 10am to 6:30pm. Tel 341-3831.

Combs & Hair Accessories

Ikuokaya—Traditional Japanese hair accessories; on Shijo (4th Avenue), east of Kawabata. Tel: 561-8087.

Jusan-ya—Handmade combs, hair ornaments; north side of Shijo (4th Avenue), east of Teramachi. Tel 211-0498.

Dolls (Ningyo)

Shimazu—On Takakura, south of Shijo (4th Avenue). Tel: 341-1181.

Goto Seikodo—Ceramic dolls; east side of Shinkyogoku, south of Takoyakushi. Tel 241-0859.

Fans

Miyawaki Baisen-an—Handmade fans. On the north side of Rokkaku and west of Tominokoji. Tel: 221-0181.

Kyo-sendo—Kyoto folding fans. On the east side of Higashi-no-toin, north of Shichijo 7th Avenue). Tel: 371-4151.

Knives, Swords and Tools

Kaiyodo—Samurai swords. On the south side of Oike, west of Horikawa. Tel 801-7227.

Mitsuhisa—Traditional Japanese carpentry tools; one street east of Senbon, 50 meters south of Sanjo (3rd Avenue). Tel: 841-2385.

Masudai Shoten—All kinds of tools, carpentry accessories and hardware; east side of Senbon, south of Sanjo (3rd Avenue). Tel 821-4309.

Lacquerware

Uruwashi-ya—Used lacquer ware at reasonable prices; south side of Marutamachi, east of Fuyacho. Tel 212-0043.

Monju—Fine lacquer ware; south side of Shijo (4th Avenue), east of Hanamikoji. Tel 525-1617.

Umbrellas

Kasagen—Handmade umbrellas. North side of Shijo (4th Avenue) and west of Higashioji; Tel: 561-2832.

Washi Paper

Kamiji Kakimoto—This is a world of handmade washi paper. It is on the east side of Teramachi, north of Nijo (2nd Avenue). Tel 211-3481.

Shopping Areas—Most of Kyoto's tiny specialty shops are situated in central Kyoto along Shijo Dori and in the area of Kawaramachi Dori—**dori** (*doh-ree*) means street or avenue.

The square formed by Kawaramachi Dori, Shijo Dori, Sanjo Dori, and Teramachi Dori includes two covered shopping arcades with shops selling lacquer ware, combs and hairpins, knives and swords, tea and tea-ceremony implements, etc. There are a number of art galleries and woodblock print shops in the famous Gion district (known for its geisha).

For those who can't get beyond Kyoto Station there is an underground shopping mall beneath the station.

CHAPTER 30

Shopping in Osaka

Historical Profile of Osaka

With a population of 2.5 million, Osaka is Japan's third largest and second most important city. It has been the economic powerhouse of the Kansai (Kyoto-Osaka-Kobe) region for many centuries. Formerly known Naniwa, the city was, in fact, Japan's first capital in recorded history (following which the capital was moved at the beginning of each new imperial reign until 794 when it was moved permanently to Kyoto).

In the 16th century, Hideyoshi Toyotomi, the paramount military leader of the day, chose Osaka as the location for his castle, and the city might have become Japan's capital again if another warlord Ieyasu Tokugawa had not terminated the Toyotomi lineage after Hideyoshi's death, and moved his government to distant Edo (Tokyo).

In the past, Osaka was often called the "Venice of the Orient" because of its rivers and numerous canals, and these waterways still play a significant role in the life of the city.

Osaka Landmarks

Osaka Castle
Feudal lord Hideyoshi Toyotomi had Osaka Castle (Osaka Jo) constructed in 1583 on the former site of the Ishiyama Honganji Temple, which had been destroyed 13 years earlier by his predecessor. However, a few years after Toyotomi's death in 1615, his successor, Ieyasu Tokugawa, attacked and destroyed the castle and terminated the Toyotomi lineage. The castle was rebuilt by Hidetada Tokugawa in the 1620s, but in 1665 its main tower was struck by lightening and burned down, only to be rebuilt once again.

The present ferro-concrete reconstruction of the castle was completed in 1931. Major repair work in 1997 gave the castle a more impressive look. It is now a museum that documents Hideyoshi Toyotomi's life and the history of the castle.

Minami (South) and Kita (North) Districts
Osaka has two large shopping and dining districts, and dozens of smaller ones. The two large ones are Kita (North) and Minami (South).

Minami is Osaka's most popular entertainment and shopping district, and is located around Namba Station. Its attractions include the Shinsaibashi Shopping Arcade, Amerikamura ("America Village"), Nipponbashi Den-Den Town (shopping area for discount electronics), and the colorful Dotonbori entertainment district.

Umeda Sky Building
The Umeda Sky Building is a spectacular high-rise building in the Kita district of Osaka, near Osaka and Umeda Stations. It is also known as the "New Umeda City".

The 173 meter tall building consists of two main towers which are connected with each other by the "Floating Garden Observatory" on the 39th floor. The observatory offers a great view of the city (for a small admission fee). The Takimi-koji restaurant mall, a replica of a Japanese street of the early Showa Period, is located in the first basement floor. Offices occupy most of the building's other floors.

HEP (Hankyu Entertainment Park) 5

This huge shopping complex (some 150 shops and restaurants) is distinguished by a giant ferris wheel that rises above the building and also dips below the upper floors of the mall. Shops include a number of Western brand names. HEP adjoins Osaka Station.

HEP 5's Ferris Wheel

The HRP Five Ferris Wheel rises 106 meters above the city. The lower dimensions of the wheel actually dip into the shopping mall. There are 52 gondolas, each with a four-person capacity. One lazy rotation takes 15 minutes. The entrance is on the 7th floor of HEP Five.

Tsutenkaku Tower

The Tsutekaku Tower, generally regarded as the symbol of Osaka, is 103 meters tall and offers a superb view of the whole of the city from the observation platform. It is located in the old downtown area and is surrounded by 'stand-and-eat' stalls and inexpensive clothing stores. 1-18-6 Ebisu-Higashi, Naniwa-ku.

World Trade Center Cosmo Tower

At a height of 256 meters, the World Trade Center Cosmo Tower is the tallest building in Western Japan. The 55th floor provides a 360-degree unbridled view of the city and its surroundings. There is a Sky Restaurant and a souvenir shop on the 55th floor. The WTC is at 1-14-16 Nanko-kita.

Dotonbori Gokuraku Shotengai (Indoor Theme Park)

Located near the Ebisubashi Bridge, this indoor theme park is spread over three floors. It is made in the styles of the Taisho and Showa era, replete with authentic fountains and sewers, streets and fortune tellers. The park has a multitude of small restaurants that feature the dishes for which Osaka is famous. There is also a Japanese Comedy House that has daily Manzai and Rakugo comic performances. 1-8-22 Dotonbori, Chuo-ku.

Ame-mura (America Mura)
Ame-mura *(Ah-may muu-rah)* is short for "American Town," the nickname of a   district west-southwest of Shinsaibashi Station that ostensibly recreates the feel and attractions of an American shopping district. It boasts a large collection of shops featuring American goods but the atmosphere is strictly Japanese. There are also numerous restaurants in the area. Nishi-shinsaibashi, Chuo-ku

Festivalgate
This is an amusement park for the whole family that houses numerous shops, restaurants and rides, including one of the world's fastest roller-coasters. It also features a number of hot springs for people who want to refresh themselves. It is located at 3-4-36 Ebisu-higashi, Naniwa-ku and adjoins the Dobutsuen-mae [Zoo-front] Station.

Kuchu Teien Tenbodai
At 557-feet the Kuchu Teien Tenbodai observation tower offers a complete 360-degree view of Osaka. It is located between the twin towers of the Umeda Sky building, and has been described as like something out of a sci-fi movie! You get to the observation platform via a super-fast glass elevator. It is at open from 10am to 10:30pm.

National Bunraku Theater
Osaka has been the capital for bunraku, the traditional Japanese puppet theater, for many centuries. Its popularity grew here during the Edo Period when puppetry (like kabuki) was a form of art entertainment for the common public rather than the nobility.

The National Bunraku Theater in Osaka is one of the few places to view the fascinating art form today. English programs and earphones are available. Performances are held six times per year for two weeks each.

Osaka Acquarium

Osaka Aquarium, also known as Kaiyukan, is regarded as Japan's best aquarium. It showcases many forms of sea-life inhabiting the Pacific Rim in a well organized and impressive way.

Marine life is displayed in 15 tanks, each representing a specific region of the Pacific Rim. The central tank, representing the Pacific Ocean, is nine meters deep and home to a whale shark, the aquarium's main attraction.

Visitors start their tour of the aquarium on the 8th floor and slowly spiral down floor by floor around the central tank. Some of the tanks stretch over several floors, making it possible to observe the animals from different depths and perspectives.

Osaka Aquarium is located in the Tempozan Harbor Village of Osaka's Port area. There is an admission fee.

Sumiyoshi Taisha

This is one of the oldest shrines in Japan. Founded in the 3rd century, before the influx of Buddhist architecture from the Asian mainland started, Sumiyoshi Taisha is one of the few shrines displaying a purely Japanese shrine architecture prototype.

The most famous of over 2,000 Sumiyoshi shrines in Japan, the Sumiyoshi Taisha enshrines kami (Shinto gods) believed to protect travelers, fishermen and sailors on the sea.

The shrine is in southern Osaka, adjoining Sumiyoshi Taisha Station on the Nankai Main Line. From Nankai Namba Station, the train ride takes less than 10 minutes by local train (futsu densha). Express trains on the line do not stop at Sumiyoshi Taisha Station, which can also be reached by the Hankai Tramway.

Osaka, founded around 683 A.D. and the first imperial capital of Japan until the late 700s, was Japan's largest purely commercial city for many centuries, and still today lives up to its name and reputation. Its large number of shopping streets, arcades and underground shopping malls are one of the most distinctive features of modern Japan.

For shopping, dining and entertainment purposes, Osaka is usually divided in to two large areas—**Kita** *(Kee-tah)* or North; and **Minami** *(Me-nah-me)* or South. Within these two areas are an amazing array of shopping districts and streets that include the **Umeda** *(Uu-may-dah)*, **Shinsaibashi** *(Sheen-sie-bah-she)*, **Namba** *(Nahm-bah)* and **Tennoji** *(Tane-no-jee)* districts, and over a dozen famous "shopping streets."

The most prominent of the shopping thoroughfares include **Mido-Suji**, **Shinsaibashi-Suji**, **Yotsubashi-Suji**, and **Naniwa-Suji**. [Suji *(Sue-jee)* translates as boulevard or avenue.]

Osaka's main shopping districts can be roughly divided into four general areas: **Umeda** *(Uu-may-dah)*, **Namba** *(Nahm-bah)*, **Shinsaibashi** *(Sheen-sie-bah-she)* and **Tennoji** *(Tane-no-jee)*. The area surrounding Namba and Shinsaibashi is especially well known for its typical Osaka flavor.

Umeda has seven mall complexes, four underground malls and three main shopping arcades. Malls range from HEP Navio and its collection of top class fashion boutiques to Loft Umeda, a place to purchase handy interior goods and sundries.

Whity Umeda is ranked as the largest underground shopping mall in Japan. Spreading out under the streets of Umeda, it is one of the major gateways to Osaka. The mall is divided into three zones, and all concourses are lined with restaurants, boutiques and novelty shops. Nearby are the department stores Hankyu, Hanshin and Daimaru.

Dia Mor Osaka, another underground shopping mall, is located west of Whity Umeda and spreads out in the shape of a diamond, from which it gets its name. It links Nishi Umeda (west side) with Higashi Umeda (east side). Its ceilings are so high and its concourses so wide it is easy to forget that you are in an underground center. There are over 70 boutiques, restaurants and art galleries in the mall.

Umeda's extensive system of underground malls that link its seven railway and subway stations, provide for comfortable shopping even in inclement weather.

One of the most popular shopper destinations in this district is Multimedia Umeda, Yodobashi Camera's huge central Osaka outlet. It is a virtual department store of electronic and electrical consumer items.

Do-Chika Shopping Center

The Dojima Underground Shopping Center, or "Do-Chika" as it is called, is another of Osaka's subterranean shopping areas enhanced with natural outside light, flowing fountains and a pleasant, relaxing ambience. It is Osaka's third oldest underground mall, and houses dozens of shops and restaurants, and a bookstore. The mall caters to local residents as well as visitors, and is definitely a place to go for atmosphere as well as shopping.

Hankyu Sanbangai Shopping Center

The unique Hankyu Sanbangai shopping complex in the Hankyu Railway Umeda Terminal Building is one of the largest shopping centers in Osaka. It has two floors above ground and two beneath filled with a variety of some 300 shops from cafes to brand name boutiques. Each floor is divided into blocks such as "Apparel Town," "Book Town," and "Toy and Electronics Town."

In the "River Town" block on the second floor basement there is an artificial river three meters wide that flows through the center of the floor. Many people throw coins into the river (the way tourists toss coins into Trevi Fountain in Rome). On the "Toy and Electronics Town" floor there is a large 12-meter waterfall that flows down from the second floor above.

Hankyu Entertainment Park (HEP) Shopping Center

HEP Navio is a collection of 130 top-class young fashion boutiques and other shops like Polo Ralph Lauren, Muji and Sanrio. There are also restaurants and a cinema complex.

HEP Five is large shopping complex with 153 specialty shops, such as Snoopy Town Shop and Disney Store, geared for young people. The gigantic whale art object in the lobby is a landmark of the facility. HEP Five also has one of Osaka's newest symbols—a bright red giant Ferris wheel on its roof. The Ferris wheel will lift you 106 meters above the ground for a spectacular view of the city.

Osaka's Famed Electronics Town

Known as Den-Den Town, this famous shopping district claims to offer the best selection and prices for electronic products and electrical appliances in the Kansai [Kyoto, Osaka, Kobe] area. There are more than 200 specialty shops in the so-called town, selling computers, PC equipment, cameras, portable stereos and other electrical and electronic items, all competing fiercely to deliver the lowest prices.

Den-Den Town is about a two-minute walk from Nipponbashi Station on the Sennichimae Subway Line. It is often described as being a mile-long shopping paradise for electric and electronic buffs.

Another major outlet for cameras and electronic products in Osaka is the Osaka branch of the Yodobashi Camera chain, adjoining the JR Osaka Station. With over 20,000 square meters of floor space, this is one of the largest shopping complexes in Western Japan.

In addition to the latest electronic goods and computer equipment at discount prices, the complex contains restaurants, boutiques and internet cafes.

Department Stores in Osaka

Osaka has six large department stores. The Hankyu Department Store in Umeda offers high-class international fashion boutiques and a wide selection of products for all ages on its ten floors.

The Hanshin Department Store, also in Umeda, has a large selection of fresh seafood and produce in its extensive basement floor, with fashion and interior items on its six other floors. It also contains an official Hanshin Tigers shop that sells sanctioned sporting goods and souvenirs with the official logo of the popular local professional baseball team.

Daimaru operates two department stores in Osaka. The Daimaru Umeda Department Store is located above JR Osaka Station. The art deco flavored Daimaru Shinsaibashi Department Store is on Mido-Suji Avenue.

The Osaka branch of Takashimaya, one of Japan's oldest

department store chains, is in Namba. It features brand name shops, imported cosmetics and fragrances, and interior furnishings.

Mitsukoshi Department Store's Osaka Branch maintains the elegant atmosphere of its flagship stores in Tokyo's Ginza and Nihonbashi.

The Kintetsu Abeno Department Store is in Tennoji. Its 11 floors have shops with a wide selection of fresh food, fashion, antiques and toys.

Namba City, Namba Walk, Nan-Nan Town

Comprising some of the key shopping attractions in the Minami Area, these three underground shopping malls are all connected to each other and are landmarks of the district.

Located under Nankai Railway's Namba Terminal, Namba City has some 300 fine boutiques, brand stores and interior stores in two complexes. It also has a 20-meter high rocket object which Osakans use as a landmark, since it can be seen from the 2nd floor basement and since it stands up to two stories above ground and outside.

Running roughly perpendicular to Namba City is Namba Walk, opened in 1970. Once called "Niji-no-Machi" (Rainbow Town), this 800-meter shopping street is accessible from six railway stations, both subway and JR, and is the main shopping mall in the Minami Area. Another 300 shops are housed here, including clothing shops, general stores, and restaurants.

Between Namba City and Namba Walk is Nan-nan Town. This mall was the first large-scale underground commercial complex in Japan, built in 1957, and its completion led to the sudden rise of similar shopping centers all over the country. Nan-nan Town is full of casual shopping and eating establishments. It was renovated in 1974.

Ebisu Bashi Suji Shopping Street

This street is named after the approach to Imamiya Ebisu Shrine. It is a shopping area that has maintained its past while also attracting young people, and setting the trends of each era.

Its covered arcade runs between the front of Takashimaya Department Store in Namba and the Dotombori district. It is filled with shopping malls, markets and flea markets, food stalls, restaurants, stands, etc., and has a fun, eclectic mixture of old and fashionable shops.

Osaka's Crysta Nagahori is one of Japan's largest underground shopping malls, with an area of 81,800 square meters. It's an amazing subterranean city of light and water, built in 1997 and designed in the image of the river that once flowed here. Its glass ceiling has water streaming over it as a reminder of days now past. The mall receives sunlight from the street above, and along with the flowing water, makes it seem like you are anything but underground.

Crysta Nagahori has over 100 trendy fashion shops and eateries arranged into four "towns." It is directly connected to five railway and subway stations, and a new underground traffic network spreads from Nagahori-Dori above it.

Shinsaibashi and Namba offer virtually unlimited shopping at their four mall complexes and four underground malls. The newest mall is Namba Parks, with a selection of more than 100 specialty shops and restaurants. Namba's underground malls are filled with fashionable boutiques.

The 600-meter long Shinsaibashi-Suji Shopping Street, which runs east to Mido-Suji Avenue, is the most famous shopping area of Osaka. One of the symbols of Osaka, it was already an established shopping area in the Edo Period almost 400 years ago, and it still bustles with people today, day or night, regardless of the weather.

In the roofed arcade, 180 shops of all kinds and for all ages line the street: traditional kimono tailors, western clothing and footwear retailers, restaurants and fast food outlets, jewelers, and boutiques featuring the latest fashions.

Many of the world's most famous designers have boutiques

along Mido-Suji Avenue, which resembles New York's 5th Avenue or Paris' Champs Elysee. Among these brands are Chanel, Hermes, Louis Vuitton and Cartier. The street attracts more shoppers and strollers than Tokyo's famed Ginza. High-class boutiques and brand shops can also be found in many shopping malls in Osaka and in leading hotel arcades.

Den Den Town (Electric-Electronic town) is the Kansai's largest electrical appliance shopping district, and comparable to Tokyo's famed Akihabara district.

The low prices and vast assortment of goods draw crowds day-in and day-out. The main street, 800 meters long, stretches from Nippombashi 3-Chome to Ebisucho, and is packed with home appliance and electronic shops, as well as shops carrying parts. Bargaining for discounts is the rule.

Nearby Doguyasuji Street is also an interesting place to check out. Shops there specialize in kitchen equipment and tableware. Also nearby, "**Osaka's Kitchen**" (*Kuromon Market*) is made up of a cluster of streets with dozens of shops selling kitchen and restaurant equipment.

Another street in this district is known as Nipponbashi Shoe Wholesaler Street. A large collection of shops on another street in the vicinity is known as "Doll Town."

"Korean Town" is also located in this area, along with "Okinawa Town".

To see how the Japanese shop for everyday things stroll down Tenjimbashisuji. It is the longest street of its kind in the country, and is both a sight to see and feel. For most visitors, it is far more interesting than Tokyo's famed Ginza. Nearby Sembayashi is famous for its bargain prices.

For bargain shoppers, there are the flea markets at Ohatsu Tenjin Shrine and the Daishie market at Shitennoji Temple, which specialize in antiques.

There are two factory outlet malls in Osaka: the Tsurumi Hanaport Blossom with its wholesale flower market and mall stocked with popular sports and casual goods; and Mare in the Asia & Pacific Trade Center (ATC). The ATC itself is also filled with gourmet restaurants, international gift shopping and amusement facilities.

Amerika Mura

America Mura, in the Namba/Shinsaibashi district is a haven for young people. It boasts many specialty shops, boutiques and art galleries, and since 1980, it has been where Osaka's free-minded youths have set local fashion trends.

On the weekends, the district is alive with street perform-ances and a flea market. It is five minutes on foot from Namba and Shinsaibashi stations (Subway Midosuji Line, Nagahori Tsurumi Ryokuchi Line).

Osaka Garden City

One of the news shopping facilities in Osaka is called Herbis Osaka, also known as Osaka Garden City, and near West Umeda. It consists of a shopping mall, a multipurpose hall, a luxury hotel, and high-grade intelligent offices.

Osaka Business Park

Osaka Business Park (OBP) is a complex of modern high-rise buildings which form a focal point of news, culture and busi-ness in Osaka.

In the park's International Market Place (IMP) there are some 60 restaurants and shops featuring goods from all over the world, including shops selling British sundries and shops specializing in museum reproductions.

Yoroppa Mura

Yoroppa (meaning "Europe") Mura is the more elegant district east of Shinsaibashi. The main street is paved with cobble stones and lined with British-style lanterns. Seasonal flower displays give the district a romantic air.

Visitors can enjoy window shopping, or drinks at any of the cafes or bars. Night time, the area is full of pleasure-seekers. It is five minutes on foot from Namba and Shinsaibashi stations (Subway Midosuji Line, Nagahori Tsurumi Ryokuchi Line).

Fashion Boutiques

Many of the world's most famous designers have opened boutiques in Osaka's the chic and bustling Kita and Minami wards, especially along the Mido-Suji Avenue, which resembles New York's 5th Avenue or Paris' Champs Elysee.

Among these brands are Chanel, Hermes, Louis Vuitton and Cartier. High-class boutiques and brand shops can also be found in many shopping malls in Osaka and in leading hotel arcades.

Two department stores are located on Mido-Suji Avenue. The Daimaru Shinsaibashi Department Store has art deco ornaments and fixtures. The Takashimaya Department Store sits on the street's southern end.

Tenno Temple Area Shopping

An older region enjoying an enduring legacy from its past, the Tennoji Area has transformed itself into a fashionable shopping place with the opening of new stores and shopping malls. Tennoji Mio and Hoop are two malls with a fine selection of stores.

The Kintetsu Abeno Department Store has everything from fashion and antiques to fresh groceries. And there is the popular Avetica underground shopping mall, mentioned earlier.

Duty Free Shopping

Duty free shopping is available at certain stores in Osaka. The Duty Free Shop at Kansai International Airport has a wide selection of designer fragrances and cosmetics, brand name jewelry and fashion accessories, liquor and tobacco.

Avic Duty Free Stores can be found at the airport and in Umeda. There are also duty-free electronics stores located in Nippombashi Den-Den (Electric and Electronic Appliances) Town.

The huge Osaka Station in Minami Ward has shopping to suit anyone's needs. Major department stores, brand name designer fashions, exotic boutiques, trendy shops, shopping malls filled with interesting stores and themed shopping arcades all come together to make up a Minami-style shopping experience.

Osaka City Air Terminal (OCAT)

The Osaka City Air Terminal (OCAT), where airline passengers can check in before getting to the airport, is above JR Namba station. If you're heading to the Kansai International Airport, you can take care of your boarding procedures and baggage here. A limousine bus will take you to the airport in about 50 minutes.

Inside OCAT there is a World Travel Information Station, as well as Internet and video-on-demand services. Also, government tourist bureaus from most countries have offices here. Between the first underground floor and the fifth floor there are shops and restaurants with everything from fashion apparel to books, CDS and sports items.

Osaka Bay Area Shopping

As with Kita and Minami wards in Osaka, shopping makes up an important part of the facilities in Osaka's Bay Area. Universal City Walk, a shopping complex located outside the Universal Studios Japan main gate, has many shops and restaurants that add to the theme park's fun and excitement.

The Tempozan Market Place is a multi-faceted entertainment complex with fashion and variety shops. The Asia-Pacific Trading Center (ATC) has two shopping areas.

The International Trade Mart has **Mare** (*Mah-ray*), a fashion outlet mall. The O's Wing in the mall has shops and restaurants with an international flavor.

One of the more prominent duty-free computer outlets in Osaka is **Mercantile Co., Ltd.** on the 8th floor of Maya Bldg. #1 at 1–2–7 Minami Honmacho, Chuo Ku. The store does system repairs and upgrades. It is closed on weekends and national holidays.

Yodobashi Camera

Yodobashi Camera is not just a "camera shop." It is a huge electronics department store that carries just about everything digital and electronic—and is an excellent choice if you do not have time to go to Den Den Town.

The Osaka branch of this amazing store is in Umeda, on the north side of the JR Osaka Station and opposite the Hotel New Hankyu. It is open daily from 9:30am to 9pm.

Sofmap (Cameras and Electronics)

Another major Umeda outlet for digital cameras, computers and accessories is the Osaka branch of Sofmap, located near the west end of JR Osaka Station. In addition to new products, this Sofmap outlet also deals in second-hand products and has an on-site computer repair clinic. It is open daily from 11am to 9:30pm.

Japan Folk Crafts
(Nihon Kogeihin Mingei Fukyubu)

This large shop features folk crafts, including ceramics, basketry, paper goods, toys and textiles collected from all over Japan. It is located at 4-7-15 Nishi-Tenma, near the Umeshin East Hotel (and is within walking distance of the U.S. Consulate office in Osaka. It is open Monday through Saturday from 10am to 5:30pm.

Snoopy Town Shop

A big portion of the merchandise in this large colorful shop is based on the famous Peanuts comic strip characters, and primarily appeals to the young, but it is patronized by teens and parents who are able to browse through a vast array of miscellaneous items that includes accessories and clothing. It is located at 5-15 Kakuta-cho in Kita-ku, and is on the fourth floor of the huge HEP Five complex. (HEP stands for Hankyu Entertainment Park.)

Sony Plaza

The Osaka branch of this nationwide chain is located in the 4th floor of the huge HEP Five complex at 5-15 Kakuda-cho in Kita-ku. Like its sister shops in Tokyo and elsewhere in Japan this Sony Plaza carries a variety of stuffed animals, gift items, games and other miscellaneous things. It is open from 11am to

9pm and is closed on the third Thursday of every month. It accepts most credit cards.

ATC (Asia & Pacific Trade Center)

The Asia & Pacific Trade Center, located in the Cosmo Square area on **Osaka's Sakishima** *(Nanko)* Island, is both a business and a pleasure venue. A world-class international wholesale trade complex filled with shops and extensive business information, it is also the key facility in the Foreign Access Zone (FAZ) and the Comprehensive Bonded Area, which allows for efficient import activities and procedures.

There are two large shopping facilities in the ATC. One is called O's and the other is called ITM or International Trade Mart. The O's building offers gourmet restaurants, international gift shopping and amusement facilities. ITM houses the outlet store MARE and the international trade market, which deals in both domestic and international goods. It also houses special event and exhibit spaces, such as the ATC Eco Green Plaza.

This spectacular complex is located at 2-1-10 Nanko-kita in, Suminoe-ku. It adjoins the OTS Trade Center-Mae subway station (exit No.2) on the Chuo Line.

The Loft

The Loft is a large building chocked full of colorful and trendy shops that cater to the younger set and to bargain shoppers looking for personal and gift items—which they have in a seemingly endless variety. The 6th floor is a general bookstore while the 7th floor is devoted entirely to music. There is a small movie theater in the basement. It is located at 16-7 Chayama-cho in Kita-ku, is open from 11am to 8pm, and is closed on some Wednesdays.

Little Korea

The area surrounding Tsuruhashi (JR Tsuruhashi, Sennichi Mae Subway and Kintetsu Tsuruhashi stations) has long been known for its numerous Korean restaurants, produce markets and shops and is generally known as "Little Korea." It attracts large numbers of people who are into Korean food and Korean arts and crafts.

Tempozan Marketplace (Osaka Harbor)

This harbor-front place is a 3-story shopping and entertainment complex that has a comprehensive art gallery and over 90 international shops (as well as a nightclubs and restaurants). It has a public events arena that also attracts large numbers of people to the area. It is located on Kaigan-dori (Beach-front Road) in Tempozan Village, and is open from 11am to 8pm. Access is via the Chuo Subway Line that goes on to Universal Studios.

Osaka's spectacular Suntory Museum and the Osaka Aquarium are also located in Tempozan Village.

Spotaka (Sports Department Store)

This is the largest sporting goods store in Osaka—10 floors of everything you can image, plus some. Each of the ten floors has its own "product theme," making finding what you want much easier. It is located at 2-5-9 Nishi-Shinsaibashi in Chuo Ward, one of Osaka's premiere shopping districts, and is open from 11am to 8pm. [Spotaka is short for "Sports Takahashi." The owner's name is Takahashi.] The nearest train station is Shinsaibashi Station.

Gare Osaka

Gare Osaka is another sports superstore, located at 3-1-1 Kakuda-cho in Kita-ku, not far from Osaka Station. The store carries virtually everything you can image in the way of sports equipment and accessories, with an emphasis on bicycles. It also features a wide range of casual and outdoor clothing from such famous companies as Mont-bell and Patagonia. The store is open from 11am to 8:30pm, and accepts most credit cards.

Mandarake

Comic books and magazines are a big thing in Japan, and this main Osaka branch of the Mandarake chain is said to be the biggest comic book store in the country. It actually looks and acts more like a comic book warehouse, with row upon row of books, magazines, posters and other kinds of artwork for children as well as adult men and women. Some of the items qualify as collectibles.

The huge store is located at 9-28 Doyama-cho in Kita-ku. It is closed on Sundays and Mondays. The nearest train station is Osaka Station.

Virgin Megastore

Located on the 5th floor of the Hankyu Entertainment Park (HEP) this huge CD, video, DVD and other music-video accessories store also has a large collection of music magazines, including most of the famous titles, domestic and foreign. It is open from 11am to 9pm. It is with a short walk of Osaka Station (at 5-15 Kakuda-cho, Kita-ku).

HMV (CD Superstore)

On the 8th floor of the **OPA Shinsaibashi Building** (1-4-3 Nishi-Shinsaibashi), HMV is one of Japan's many music superstores. In addition to an enormous collection of Japanese and Western CDs, the story has a large number of listening booths for the convenience of customers. It is open from 11am to 9pm, and closed on Tuesdays and Thursdays. Shinsaibashi Station is the nearest station.

DJ's Store

If you are into vinyl records, you will love this place. It has over 2,500 records in a variety of genres, many of which are rare collectibles. (The owner buys as well as sells.) It is located in Nishi-Shinsaibashi (2-17-13), near the huge OPA shopping building. The nearest station is Shinsaibashi Station. Call for hours. Tel 06-6213-33423.

Fashion/Clothing

Anna Sui
New York fashion store for women.
Big Step 1F, 1-6-14 Nishi-Shinsaibashi, Chuo-ku

ATC Town Outlet Mare
Bayside Shopping Center
2-1-10 Nanko-kita, Suminoe-ku
ATC Building, ITM wing

55DSL
Sturdy, urban wear.
5-15 Kakuda-cho, Kita-ku
HEP Five 5F (Hankyu Entertainment Park Building)

Eddie Bauer
Famous brand-name casual wear.
2-1-22 Shinsaibashi-suji, Chuo-ku

Gap
World leader in casual clothing.
5-15 Kakuda-cho, Kita-ku
HEP Five 2F

L. L. Bean (Umeda)
Famous brand-name casual wear.
Osaka Marubiru 2F
1-9-20 Umeda, Kita-ku

Mary Quant
Quality cosmetics and accessories.
5-15 Kakuda-cho, Kita-ku
Hep Five 3F

Mujirushi Ryohin
Items for your home, wardrobe.
7-10 Kakuda-cho, Kita-ku
HEP Navio 5F

Musee de Dragon
Designer clothing from around the world.
1-9-20 Umeda, Kita-ku
Osaka Maru Building B1

Patagonia
Rugged clothing.
2-10-34, Nishi-Shinsaibashi, Chuo-ku

Polo Ralph Lauren
Some of the best classy clothing.
7-10 Kakuda-cho, Kita-ku
HEP Navio 1F

Stussy
Brand-name fashion anchor.
5-15 Kakuda-cho, Kita-ku
HEP Five 5F

Kooks & Chelica
Cute women's clothing.
Big Step BF2
1-6-14 Nishi-Shinsaibashi

United Arrows
Fantastic range of clothing.
Big Step 1F
1-6-14 Nishi-Shinsaibashi, Chuo-ku

United Colors of Benetton
Stylish, casual line of clothing for women.
1-32 Chaya-machi, Kita-ku

X-LARGE
Youth casual wear.
HEP Five 5F
5-15 Kakuda-cho, Kita-ku

CHAPTER 31

Shopping in Kobe/Sannomiya

The two most impressive shopping districts in the port city of Kobe are Motomachi and Sannomiya. There is also a large shopping mall called San Chika Town that begins in front of Sannomiya Station in the middle of Kobe.

Daimaru department store is near Motomachi Station, and Sogo is at Sannomiya Station.

Kobe's "China Town" (**Nankin Machi**/*Nahn-keen Mah-chee*), is relatively small, but it has several shops featuring Chinese merchandise (and a number of Chinese restaurants). It is within walking distance of both Motomachi Station and Sannomiya Station (ten minutes from the latter).

Santica Town

This underground shopping mall, located in Sannomiya, an upscale district adjoining downtown Kobe on the north side, has 120 shops and 30 restaurants. It extends for several blocks beneath Flower Road south from Sannomiya Station. The mall is closed on the third Wednesday in each month.

CHAPTER 32

Shopping in Hiroshima

One of the premiere shopping areas in Hiroshima is an underground mall near Kamiyacho that is called **Share-O**. Despite what it looks like, "share" is a Japanese word pronounced *shah-ray*, and meaning neat, cool, fashionable.

There are over 100 stores in the impressive mall (opened in 2006), some 80 of which sell fashion goods. The others sell miscellaneous merchandise that is typical in Japanese stores, including food items. There are also restaurants and drinking places.

CHAPTER 33

Shopping in Nagasaki

Nagasaki has the usual collection of gift and souvenir shops that cater to both domestic and foreign travelers. Here are some shops that cater to visitors.

Yogashikobo Speciality Store, 14–11 Hanaoka-machi, Nagasaki.

Nookie, 11–6 Hamanomachi, Nagasaki. Fashion/ Clothing.

Futabaya Specialty Store, 8–12 Shinchi-machi, Nagasaki.

CHAPTER 34

Shopping in Kagoshima

Local Kagoshima products include **oshima tsumugi** (*oh-she-mah t'suu-muu-ghee*), a beautiful silk made into such items as clothing, handbags, and wallets; **shochu** (*show-chuu*), an alcoholic drink made from such ingredients as sweet potatoes and drunk either on the rocks or mixed with boiling water.

Other famous Kagoshima products include furniture, statues, chests made from yaku cedar, and Satsuma pottery, Kagoshima's most famous product. It has been produced in the area since the mid–1600s.

Satsuma pottery comes in two styles: black and white. White Satsuma pottery is more elegant and was used by former lords; black pottery was used by the townspeople in everyday life.

A good place to shop for local items is the Display Hall of Kagoshima Products, downtown in the Sangyo Kaikan Building (the same building housing the Kagoshima Prefectural Tourist Office) at 9-1 Meizan-cho.

The hall is open daily 9 a.m.–5 p.m., but closed on the 1st and 3rd Sunday of the month. The shop offers tinware, handmade knives, Satsuma pottery, glassware, oshima tsumugi, yaku cedar, shochu, and other locally made items.

The most famous food product of Kagoshima (the one all Japanese tourists must buy before returning home) is

karukan (*kah-rue-kahn*), a spongy white cake made from rice, with Chinese and Korean origins.

The most famous maker of **karukan** today is Akashiya, 4–16 Kinseicho, which began selling the cakes in the 18th century. It is located behind the Yamakataya department store.

Although cakes made from beans and other ingredients are now available in Kagoshima, old-timers insist that only the plain white ones are the real thing.

Kagoshima residents like to claim that Japan's industrial revolution started there because 17 young men from the Satsuma clan broke the Tokugawa Shogunate's 200-year plus ban on foreign travel by going abroad to bring back technology and science from the West.

The daring young students are commemorated by a large statue outside the city's main train station.

CHAPTER 35

Shopping in Naha, Okinawa

Okinawa's culture differs significantly from that of mainland Japan, because it was an independent kingdom for hundreds of years and was more influenced by the cultures of Southeast Asia.

Okinawa's arts and crafts reflect this cultural difference, making them especially popular among domestic as well as international travelers. Among items that are unique to Okinawa: Ryukyu glass items, Tuboya pottery and a unique style of lacquerware.

Probably the best place for visitors in Naha to shop is Naha Main Place, a complex of some 70 shops that feature virtually everything made in and available in Okinawa.

The complex is located in what amounts to Naha's new center, located on land once occupied by American military forces. The shopping center is owned by a large Japanese corporation that has shops all over Okinawa.

(There is a restaurant zone in the complex, including a Starbucks Coffee Shop, as well as a ¥100 Plaza.)

Okinawa opened its first two duty-free shops for domestic flights inside Naha airport in May, 2002.

Japan's nation's first duty-free shop to operate outside an airport opened in the Omoromachi district of Naha in 2004. The store, DFS Galleria, was established under the Law on Special Measures for the Promotion and Development of Okinawa.

The three-story DFS Galleria shopping center is packed with

foreign designer bags, wristwatches and cosmetics. The store is open to domestic passengers departing from Okinawa, who are required to show boarding passes when purchasing an item.

Main Shopping Districts/Streets in Okinawa

Mihama American Village—This facility is a restaurant and retail store complex with a Ferris wheel, multi-screen movie theater, and shops and restaurants featuring local products.

Kokusai Street in Naha—The biggest and oldest shopping street on Okinawa, this one-mile long strip is lined with about 600 shops.

Shin-Toshin—A former United States military housing area that is now a bustling new "town" in Naha, it includes San-A Main Place (mentioned above), Okinawa's largest shopping mall; a Sports Depot, Toys "R" Us; and a variety of shops, stylish restaurants and coffee houses.

Plaza House Shopping Center—This is the place to go for traditional Okinawan products such as Ryukyu lacquer ware, Ryukyu glassware, Okinawan dyed and woven textiles and Okinawan health foods. A three-story mall offers clothing, compact discs, jewelry and Japanese folk crafts.

There are a number of shops located in both of Okinawa's airport terminals, including travel goods shops, pharmacies, gift shops; newspapers and books, duty-free outlets and electronic shops.

¥100 Stores—These popular stores carry a huge variety of items, all for ¥100. The island's largest ¥100 store is in Haninsu Ginowan. Another ¥100 store called Daiso Miyazato, which has an expansive showroom, is in Okinawa City's Miyazato district.

CHAPTER 36

Shopping in Sendai

Sendai is the main city in the Tohoku or northern district of Honshu (Japan's main island), and was long known as a frontier town famed for the horses it provided to the Tokugawa Shogunate government from 1603 to 1868.

Present-day Sendai is famous for its wide, tree-lined streets (it is popularly known as **Mori no Miyako** (*Moe-ree no Me-yah-koe*), or "City of Trees"), the prevailing cowboy attitude of its inhabitants, and its extensive shopping facilities.

Altogether the city has six major shopping malls, including Ichiban-Cho Sun Mall, a covered street that begins a short distance from the west side of Sendai Station. In addition to hundreds of clothing boutiques and shops it also has a number of department stores. An elevated pedestrian walkway leads to covered shopping mall.

Chuo Dori (*Chuu-oh Doe-ree*), Central Avenue, (also known as Clis Road) is the city's traditional shopping street. Another popular shopping venue in Sendai is the first four floors of the towering aer Building (the tallest building in the region), on the north side of Sendai Station. [Sendai Station actually consists of two terminals connected by an undergdound passageway.]

Like all regions of Japan, the Sendai area has its traditional **meibutsu** (*may-ee-boot-sue*), or "famous products". These include:

Kokeshi (*koe-kay-she*) dolls carved from dogwood and maple, with mountainous areas in the region having their own specialties, such as Naruko and Togatta, whose dolls have their own unique expressions.

Tansu (*tahn-sue*) chests characterized by the application of very thin coasts of lacquer which highlight the grain of the zelkova wood, along with splendid decorations of its hand-beaten metalwork. Sendai's **tansu** have long been prized as folk furniture.

Tamamushi (*tah-mah-muu-she*) lacquereware, referring to a lacquer technique that is used for flower vases, letter cases, bowls for sweets, smoking sets and others things in which silver powder is sprinkled under a layer of lacquer, emitting a soft, jewel-like glow, like the colorful wings of a **tamamushi** (beetle).

Tsutsumi (*T'sue-t'sue-me*) earthen dolls famous for their coloring, and is often compared with the noted **fushimi** (*fuu-she-me*) dolls of Kyoto. Noh masks, sumo wrestlers and horses are among the many **tsutsumi** doll motifs.

These products, and more, are available in the usual large collection of shops in and around Sendai Station, in hotel arcades, and in the city's primary shopping streets.

The Chinese Come

In 2005 one of China's largest development companies (Zhongrui Caituan) began construction of a four-acre shopping mall in Sendai—nine stories above ground and one below; featuring shops and Chinese restaurants. It is one of the most spectacular shopping facilities in northern Japan.

CHAPTER 37

Shopping in Sapporo

Probably the most distinctive thing about tourist shopping in Sapporo, the northern island of Hokkaido's largest city, is that many gift and souvenir shops feature items made by the island's native Ainus—a Caucasoid people who were the original inhabitants of most of the Japanese islands, particularly the central and northern regions.

Sapporo has a variety of stores ranging from ¥100 shops and discount stores to specialty stores and high-class department stores. Sapporo Factory, the former site of the Sapporo brewery, houses dozens of shops and a cinema complex. The Odori Park and Sapporo Station areas also have several department stores.

Long-established department stores such as Mitsukoshi and Marui are located near Odori Park, while Seibu, Tokyu and Daimaru department stores are in the Sapporo Station area. The Sapporo Station building itself is a huge shopping zone with a cinema complex and many specialty stores.

Odori Park—Sapporo's Odori Park, which extends for 1.5 km east-west in the center of the city, is an urban oasis. Decorated with fountains, sculptures and flower beds, the park serves as a site for the city's Snow Festival in February, its Lilac Festival in May, the Yosakoi Soran Festival in June, and the Summer Festival in summer. It is also converted into a giant summertime Beer Garden.

Underground Shopping Malls

The there are two underground shopping malls in the center of the city that are meccas for shoppers: the Sapporo Underground Shopping Mall and the Apia Mall.

The Sapporo Mall has two sections or "towns"—Pole Town, which runs north and south between Odori Station and Susukino; and Aurora Town, which runs east and west and links Odori Station with the TV Tower complex.

Apia Underground Mall begins at the South Exit of Sapporo Station, and centers on "Sun Square." There are 115 shops around the Square, most of them specializing in fashion wear and gourmet foods.

Sapporo Station also has an underground shopping area, where many boutiques and other specialty stores offer the latest fashion items. The main Sapporo underground shopping mall extends from Odori Park to Susukino—a godsend during the cold winter months.

The Tanuki Koji shopping arcade, which stretches eight blocks from east to west, has dozens of clothing shops, cafes and ramen shops. This area has a nostalgic atmosphere because it retains the city's old Shogun era landscapes.

CHAPTER 38

Shopping in Fukuoka

The metropolitan area of Fukuoka on the northern end of Kyushu Island is not as well known abroad as other Japanese cities, but for nearly two thousand years it was Japan's gateway to Korea, China and the rest of Asia, serving as the country's leading seaport and a major commercial and industrial center. It remains today one of the country's largest commercial/industrial areas.

There are three noted shopping areas in Fukuoka: **Tenjin** *(Tane-jeen)*, **Hakata** *(Hah-kah-tah)* and **Chuo Ku** *(Chuu-oh Kuu)*.

Tenjin is Fukuoka's largest shopping area. Its main shopping districts include Keiyaki-dori [Keiyaki Street], the chic Daimyo area, along with such major retail outlets as Tenjin Core, IMS, Vivre, Underground, and Iwataya. There are also several shopping centers like the Tenjin Chikagai [Tenjin Underground Shopping Mall] which runs underground next to the Tenjin subway station, as well as a large mall called Canal City, which has numerous clothing stores, restaurants and rare "character shops" like an Osame Tezuka's and Studio Ghibli's goods shop.

Department stores in the Tenjin area include IMS, Solaria, Mitsukoshi, Daimaru and Iwataya Z-side. Tenjin has also long been known for its **yatai** *(yah-tie)* or "street stalls," selling the area's famous ramen noodles.

Hakata [which was an independent city until recent times]

is best known for its Hakata dolls, Hakata-ori textiles, Yame Fukushima funerary alters, Agano Ware pottery, Hakata ramen, and other traditional handicrafts.

Chuo Ku (Central Ward) is the business heart of the city, with block-after-block of hotels, office buildings, department stores, specialty shops and restaurants. Many visitors never get beyond this downtown area, but it is in Tenjin and Hakata that one finds the most traditional items. If you are pressed for time, the area around Hakata Station has a collection of boutique and craft shops that carry most of Fukuoka's most famous products.

For more shopping (and dining) details, see the city's online English-language magazine Fukuoka Now, at http://www.fukuoka-now.com/index.php. The online magazine includes detailed information about more than 50 shops in the Tenjin and Hakata areas that cater especially to visitors, with photographs of leading products.

CHAPTER 39

Outlet Malls

There are outlet malls in or on the outskirts of virtually all of Japan's larger cities, as well as in rural areas where they serve nearby towns and villages.

Most of these malls include shops catering to Japanese tourists—meaning that they carry local and regional items that visitors buy as gifts and souvenirs.

While the same items are generally available to foreign travelers in more accessible outlets, a visit to one or more outlet malls can be rewarding as a good way to experience the shopping scene and the routine of daily life in Japan.

Outlet malls in the more remote parts of Japan thus serve as introductions to the local and regional culture, and are visitor attractions within themselves.

Most of outlet malls have a variety of entertainment facilities, and on weekends and holidays, many families take their children to local malls as a combined dining, shopping and outing experience.

Foreign tourists wanting to visit an outlet mall can make arrangements through a tour company or through the concierge desk of their hotel.

CHAPTER 40

Station Shopping!

This heading does not refer to shopping for stations. It refers to the fact that there are literally thousands of railway terminals in Japan that have become major shopping centers. Some of the terminals are "built into" department stores and huge office buildings, the latter with large shopping arcades.

In addition to the shopping facilities within the station buildings, virtually every major terminal in all of Japan's cities is also surrounded by a complex of shops, restaurants and bars. In Tokyo alone, the number of station shopping areas must be around 500.

Tokyo Station Shopping

The east side of the huge, sprawling Tokyo Central Station contains dozens of shops carrying a wide range of products, from regional fruits and handicrafts to travel accessories and wearing apparel.

Visitors to Japan tend to want to get in and out of stations as quickly as possible, but when they do they miss one of the most interesting and convenient shopping places in the country. At the very least, a stroll through the aisle and concourse shopping facilities in stations is a sight worth seeing.

Shinagawa Station Shopping

One of the most impressive of the station shopping complexes in Japan is the "Atre Shinagawa Shopping Center" on the east side of Shinagawa Station in Tokyo. This center consists of a 4-story futuristic building that became a sightseeing attraction the day it opened.

The center has 21 shops featuring a variety of international themes, with one of the most impressive themes being the "New York Street Look" on the second floor—which includes an upscale delicatessen.

The third floor is a luxury food supermarket, Queen's Isetan. The fourth floor is reminiscent of an airport lounge or hotel lobby. The sophisticated mix of stores includes the first overseas branch of the famous Oyster Bar from New York's Grand Central Station.

Other major "shopping stations" in Tokyo include Hamamatsu-cho, Meguro, Shibuya, Shinjuku, Ikebukuro Ebisu and Ueno—and these are just a few of those on the Yamanote commuter loop line that encircles the heart of the city.

The same situation exits in all of Japan's major cities. The central stations (where the long-distance trains stop) as well as dozens to hundreds of local commuter stations are virtual shopping malls—including, of course, Nagoya, Kyoto, Osaka, Kobe, Hiroshima, Hakata, Nagasaki and Kagoshima.

CHAPTER 41

Airport Shopping

If you forgot or failed for any reason to do all the shopping that you wanted to do in Japan before leaving for the airport, don't be concerned. The departure areas of Japan's international airports include extensive shopping (and dining) arcades.

Shopping at Narita International Airport

Both of Narita's two terminals (about half a mile apart) have extensive shopping facilities offering virtually every souvenir and gift-type product made in Japan—all of them oriented toward departing passengers.

In Terminal 1, which consists of a South Wing and a North Wing that are connected by a Central Building, there are shops on the 4th and 5th floors of the Central Building as well as on the 4th floor of the North Wing.

These include brand name gift shops, arts and craft shops, cameras, bags, watches, pearls, books and magazines, toys, accessories, cosmetics audio visual equipment and various electrical products, travel goods, cell phones, medicines, clothes and sundries.

All of the above shops are located in areas prior to departure procedures. After you pass through Customs and Immigration there are arcades of duty-free shops featuring a wide selection of travel goods, perfumes, watches and the like—many of them imported.

In Terminal 2 the shopping areas are located in the Main Building, with shops in B1 (the first basement) and the 1st through 4th floors. There are more shops in the newer Terminal 2 than in Terminal 1, and they include a larger number of name outlets, such as Mitsukoshi Department Store, Kintetsu and Takashimaya.

After you go through Customs and Immigration in Terminal 2 there is the usual collection of Duty Free shops—in this case, in both the Main Building and the Satellite concourse where the departure lounges are located.

Narita International Airport also has a large collection of restaurants, featuring American (including a McDonald's), Chinese, Japanese, and Korean dishes, as well as many Japanized Western dishes. Virtually all of the restaurants (except for McDonald's) have replicas of their main dishes in front displays that include the name of the dish and the price.

Other facilities in both Terminals include showers and day rooms, an audio video room, a children's playroom, Internet connection rooms, post offices and clinics. There is a dental clinic in B1 of the Central Building of Terminal 1.

The showers and day rooms as well as the audio video room and children's playroom can be used only by passengers who have completed Customs and Immigration procedures.

Some visitors choose to do all of their shopping at Narita rather than cart their purchases around or ship them home in advance. Others look for things they forgot or didn't come across prior to their departure day. There are numerous shops in both terminals, both before and after you complete Immigration procedures.

Shopping at Kansai International Airport

There are over 100 shops in the Kansai International Airport (which serves Kyoto, Osaka, Kobe and the surrounding prefectures), carrying the usual handicrafts, souvenirs, gifts, and a variety of duty-free items. The adjoining Aeroplaza Shopping Mall caters to those with longer waiting periods.

A bank is located on the second floor of the terminal, while ATMS and money exchange offices are located on most floors.

(There are also 35 restaurants in Kansai International Airport, 21 of them serving Japanese dishes, including sushi and noodles. Additionally, there are 26 coffee shops and several bars, many of them offering snack items as well as alcoholic drinks.)

The architectural design of Kansai International Airport is spectacular, resulting in many domestic passengers deliberately going to the airport early in order to sightsee, dine and shop in extraordinary surroundings.

Shopping at Haneda Airport

Haneda, Japan's original international airport, located some 15 to 20 minutes from downtown Tokyo, now serves both domestic and selected international flights. The Haneda Terminal, while small in comparison with Narita and Kansai, has an impressive collection of shops and restaurants. Shopping facilities here are primarily oriented toward Japanese who are traveling in country.

Shopping at Other Airports

Shops in Japan's city and regional domestic airports, including Sapporo, Sendai, Nagoya, Osaka and Kobe, can be counted on to feature famous local and regional products, known as **meibutsu** (*may-ee-boot-sue*), "famous products," that have been popular for generations—some of them going back for more than a thousand years.

Visitors who make use of Japan's domestic airlines should not miss the opportunity to check out the **meibutsu** of the areas they visit. The products are often not available in other parts of Japan, and can often be had at bargain prices.

For example, the cost of pearls sold at the Mikimoto pearl farm near Nagoya is invariably lower than what it is in Tokyo outlets, and Japan's famous lacquerware is bound to be cheaper in Shikoku where it is made.

Like Kansai International Airport, Kobe Airport is located on a man-made island (Port Island) that is connected to the mainland by a rail and vehicular causeway, and deserves special mention because of its impressive design. Its facilities include 27 shops and restaurants.

CHAPTER 42

Shopping Online

Online shopping took off in Japan in the 1990s, and is still growing at a rapid pace. The largest "online shopping mall" in the country is called **Rakuten** (*Rah-kuu-tane*), which incorporates the meanings of "cheerful" and "optimistic", "an amusement center" and "paradise."

There are dozens of online shops offering Japanese goods of all kinds, from arts and crafts to the latest electronic devices and traditional apparel. All you have to do is go to Google and type in Japanese shops online. Several million websites will come up—out of which several hundred are well-established have good reputations, including a number offering Japanese food items.

Several of these latter online sites are maintained by retailers and wholesalers of Japanese goods outside of Japan, particularly in the United States.

One place to start is monstermarketplace.com. Others: Japan-Zone.com, GoodsfromJapan.com, and Japan-shop.com.

CHAPTER 43

Flea Markets
Shopping in Japan

There are flea markets in virtually all Japanese cities, most of them operating only on weekends and on holidays. Things typically found in flea markets include used clothing, accessories, toys, shoes, books, pottery and ironware.

In Tokyo most of the larger flea markets are organized and operated by the Tokyo Recycle Campaign Citizen's Association (03-3384-6666), and similarly named Recycle Campaign Citizen's Association (03-3226-6800).

In Osaka the Japan Garage Sale Association (06-6362-6322) and the Japan Flea Market Association (06-6531-8417) are the sponsors of most of the flea markets.

Here is a list of the oldest and largest flea markets in Tokyo and Osaka. [See the flea market guide book described below for a comprehensive list of flea markets throughout Japan.]

Flea Markets in Tokyo

Aoyama Oval Building Swap Meet
Access: Chiyoda, Ginza and Hanzomon Subway Lines; Omotesando Station. Open on the 2nd Saturday and Sunday of each month.

Ariake Jumbo Flea Market/500 Booths
Location: Rinkai Fukutoshin Ariake Minami Event Hiroba. Access: Yurikamome Line from Shimbashi, Ariake Station. Admission 300 yen. Open on most Sundays (irregular). Tel. 03-3226-6800.

Makuhari Jumbo Flea Market/300 booths
Location: Kaihin Makuhari Station North Entrance, Access: JR Keiyo Line Kaihin Makuhari Station. Free Admission. Held on irregular Sundays. Tel 03-3355-6071.

Meiji Park Flea Market
Access: JR Sendagaya Station
Open Saturdays and Sundays (irregular schedule).

Kiba Park Market
Access: Tozai Subway Line, Kiba Station. Open Saturdays and Sundays (irregular schedule). For more information, contact Tokyo Recycle Campaign Citizen's Association (03-3384-6666)

Yoyogi Park Flea Market
Access: JR Harajuku Station. Open Sundays or Saturdays (irregular schedule). Schedules and locations within the park are subject to change without notice. For more information, contact Tokyo Recycle Campaign Citizen's Association (03-3384-6666)

Flea Markets in Osaka

Osaka Business Park Flea Market
Family oriented items, antiques, and more. Location: Chuo-ku, Shiromi KDD Osaka Building. Hiroba Entrance. Access: JR Osaka Kanjo Line, Kyobashi Station. Via subway: the Nagahori Tsurumi Ryokuchi Line, Osaka Business Park Station. Free Admission. Open 1st Sunday of each month from 11am to 5pm.

Uehon machi Square Market

Location: Tennouji-ku Uehonmachi. Access: Tanimachi Subway Line, Tanimachi 9-chome Station. Also, Kintetsu Nanba Line, Uehonmachi Station. Free Admission. Open first and third Saturdays and Sundays. Also Accessible via the Nankai Honsen Line, Yoshimino-sato Station.

Nankou Flea Market (up to 300 booths)

Location: Cosmo Square. Access New Tram Tecno Port Line, Cosmo Square Station. Admission 300 yen. Open Sundays (irregular). Call the Japan Garage Sale Association for schedules: 06-6362-6322.

OCAT Flea Market (150 booths)

Location: Naniwaku Minatomachi Osaka Air City Terminal. Access: JR Namba Station.
Admission: 200yen. Open 3rd Sundays. For more information, call 06-6362-6322 (Japan Garage Sale Association) or 06-6531-8417 (Japan Flea Market Association)

Tajiri Gyokou Nichiyou Asaichi

Fresh seafood, vegetables, knives, and more. Location: Rinku Port, Tajiri Fishing Port. Open from 7a.m. to noon on Sundays. Free Admission. Tel 0724-65-0099.

Ohatsu-Tenjin Nomino-ichi

Roten Shrine Flea Market; specializes in antiques. Location: Kitaku Sonezaki Roten Jinjya Shrine.

Free Admission. Open first and third Fridays. Schedules and locations are subject to change without notice. Tel (06) 6790-3781 for current information.

For a comprehensive guide to Japan's flea markets, see Theodore Manning's Flea Markets of Japan: A Pocket Guide for Antique Buyers, available from Amazon.com.

The book covers the advantages of flea markets over antique stores, and the availability, quality and prices of antiques sold through this channel. It lists 115 flea markets throughout Japan. The heart of the book is its Things to Buy section, which gives names and descriptions for 450 antiques and artifacts, conveniently classified into 18 categories.

Lastly, the section on "flea-market Japanese" supplies the shopper with the linguistic tools to bring it all together, with a "survival kit" of over 250 shopping-related Japanese words and phrases. It also includes flea market bargaining techniques and a special section on etiquette.

CHAPTER 44

Handy Shopping Dictionary

adaptor (electrical) **adapta** (*ah-dahp-tah*)
after-shave lotion **afuta-shebu roshon**
    (*ah-fuu-tah-shay-buu roe-shoan*)
ashtray **hai-zara** (*hie-zah-rah*)
aspirin **asupirin** (*ahss-puu-reen*)

ballpoint pen **boru pen** (*boe-rue pen*)
bandage **hotai** (*hoe-tie*)
bargain **bagen** (*bah-gain*); also **seru** (*say-rue*);
    o-uridashi (*oh-uu-ree-dah-she*)
bathing suit **mizugi** (*me-zuu-ghee*)
bathrobe **basurobu** (*bah-sue-roe-buu*)
battery (car) **batteri** (*bah-tay-ree*)
battery (flashlight) **denchi** (*dane-chee*)
bedding **shingu** (*sheen-guu*)
belt **beruto** (*bay-rue-toe*)
black-and-white film **shiro-kuro firumu**
    (*she-roe-kuu-roe fee-rue-muu*)
blanket **mofu** (*moe-fuu*)
blazer **bureza** (*buu-ray-zahh*)
blouse **burausu** (*buu-rah-uu-sue*)
book **hon** (*hoan*)
book (English) **Eigo no hon** (*aa-ee-go no hoan*)

book (Japanese)
   Nihongo no hon (*nee-hoan-go no hoan*)
boot **butsu** (*boot-sue*)
bottle opener **sen-nuki** (*sane-nuu-kee*)
bow tie **cho-nekutai** (*choe-nay-kuu-tie*)
brocade **nishiki** (*nee-shee-kee*)
brooch **burochi** (*buu-roe-chee*)
broom **hoki** (*hoe-kee*)
brush **burashi** (*buu-rah-she*)
bucket **baketsu** (*bah-kate-sue*)
button **botan** (*boe-tahn*)

calculator **dentaku** (*dane-tah-kuu*)
can **kan** (*kahn*)
can opener **kan-kiri** (*kahn-kee-ree*)
canteen **suito** (*sue-e-toe*)
cap; hat **boshi** (*boe-she*)
capsule **kapuseru** (*kop-say-rue*)
cashier counter **okanjo** (*oh-kahn-joe*);
   also **o-kaikei** (*oh-kie-kay*)
cassette **kasetto** (*kah-set-toe*)
change (money) **o-tsuri** (*oh-t'sue-ree*)
clock **tokei** (*toe-kay-e*)
coat **uwagi** (*uu-wah-ghee*)
coffee cup **kohi-jawan** (*koe-hee-jah-won*);
   also **kohi-koppu** (*koehee-koe-puu*)
collar **eri** (*aa-ree*)
color **iro** (*ee-roe*)

deodorant **shoshu-zai** (*show-shuu-zie*)
department store information counter
   annai-jo (*ahn-nie-joe*);
   also **infomeshon** (*in-foo-may-shoan*)
detergent **senzai** (*sane-zie*)
develop (a photograph) **genzo** (*gane-zoe*)
dictionary **jibiki** (*iee-bee-kee*); also **jisho** (*jee-show*)

English-Japanese dictionary
Ei-Wa jiten (*aa-ee-wah jee-ten*)
Japanese-English dictionary
Wa-Ei jiten (*wah-aa-ee jee-ten*)
dinner jacket; tuxedo **takishido** (*tah-kee-shee-doe*)
discount **waribiki** (*wah-ree-bee-kee*)
20 percent discount **ni waribiki** (*nee wah-ree-bee-kee*)
30 percent discount
san waribiki (*sahn wah-ree-bee-kee*)
50 percent discount **go waribiki** (*go wah-ree-bee-kee*)
dish **sara** (*sah-rah*)
doll **ningyo** (*neen-g'yoe*)
dress **wan-pisu** (*wahn-pee-sue*)
dustcloth **zokin** (*zoe-keen*)

earring **iyaringu** (*ee-ah-reen-guu*)
enlarge (a photograph)
hiki-nobasu (*he-kee-no-bah-sue*)
envelope **futo** (*fuu-toe*)
eraser **keshi-gomu** (*kay-she-go-muu*)
evening dress
ibuningu-doresu (*ee-buu-neen-guu-doe-ray-sue*)
exchange (merchandise) **tori-kaeru** (*toe-ree-kie-rue*)
exposure meter (camera)
roshutsukei (*roe-shuu-t'sue-kay-e*)
eyedrop **me-gusuri** (*may-guu-sue-ree*)
eye liner **ai-raina** (*eye-rye-nah*)
eye shadow **ai-shado** (*eye-shah-doe*)

file **fairu** (*fie-rue*)
filter (camera) **firuta** (*fee-rue-tahh*)
fingernail clipper **tsume-kiri** (*t'sue-may-kee-ree*)
fingernail file **tsume yasuri** (*t'sue-may yah-sue-ree*)
fingernail polish **manikyua** (*mah-nee-cue-ah*)
fingernail-polish remover
manikyua rimuba (*mah-nee-cue-ah ree-muu-bah*)

first-aid kit **kyukyu-bako** (*cue-cue-bah-koe*)
flashbulb (camera) **furasshu** (*fuu-rah-shuu*)
folk craft **mingei-hin** (*mean-gay-e-heen*)
frying pan **furai-pan** (*fuu-rye-pahn*)

gaberdine **gyabajin** (*g'yah-bah-jeen*)
gauze **gaze** (*gahh-zay*)
glove **tebukuro** (*tay-buu-kuu-roe*)
glue **nori** (*no-ree*)
guidebook **gaido-bukku** (*gie-doe-buu-kuu*)

hairbrush **hea-burashi** (*hay-ah-buu-rah-she*)
hair dryer **hea-doraia** (*hay-ah-doe-rye-ahh*)
hair roller **hea-rora** (*hay-ah-roe-rah*)
half price **hangaku** (*hahn-gah-kuu*)
hammer **kanazuchi** (*kah-nah-zuu-chee*)
handbag **hando-baggu** (*hahn-doe-bah-guu*)
hand cream **hando-kurimu** (*hahn-doe-kuu-ree-muu*)
handkerchief **hankachi** (*hahn-kah-chee*)
hanging scroll **kake-jiku** (*kah-kayjee-kuu*)
hardware **kana-mono** (*kah-nah-moe-no*)
hat **boshi** (*boe-she*)
heater **sutobu** (*sue-toe-buu*)
electric heater **denki-sutobu** (*dane-kee-sue-toe-buu*)
gas heater **gasu-sutobu** (*gah-sue-sue-toe-buu*)
kerosene heater **sekiyu-sutobu** (*say-kee-yuu-sue-toe-buu*)

instruction booklet **setsumei-sho** (*sate-sue-may-show*)
iron **airon** (*aye-rone*)

jacket **jaketto** (*jah-ket-toe*)
jeans **jinzu** (*jeen-zoo*)
jewelry **hoseki** (*hoe-say-kee*)

kitchen **daidokoro** (*die-doe-koe-roe*);
   also **kicchin** (*kee-cheen*)

kitchen knife **hocho** (*hoe-choe*)
kitchen utensil
   daidokoro yohin (*die-doe-koe-roe yoe-heen*)

lace **resu** (*ray-sue*)
lacquerware **nuri-mono** (*nuu-ree-moe-no*);
   also **shikki** (*sheek-kee*)
laundry soap
   sentaku-sekken (*sane-tah-kuu sake-ken*)
laxative **gezai** (*gay-zie*)
leather **kawa** (*kah-wah*)
lens (camera) **renzu** (*rane-zuu*)
lighter **raita** (*rie-tah*)
lingerie **ranjeri** (*rahn-jay-ree*);
   also **shita-gi** (*ssh-tah-ghee*)
lining **ura** (*uu-rah*); also **ura-ji** (*uu-rah-jee*)
lipstick **kuchi-beni** (*kuu-chee-bay-nee*)
lotion **roshon** (*roe-shoan*)

made in Japan **Nihon-sei** (*Nee-hoan-say-e*)
magazine **zasshi** (*zah-she*)
map **chizu** (*chee-zuu*)

nail (finger) **tsume** (*t'sue-may*)
necklace **nekkuresu** (*neck-kuu-ray-sue*)
necktie **nekutai** (*nay-kuu-tie*)
needle **nui-bari** (*nuu-ee-bah-ree*)
newspaper **shinbun** (*sheen-boon*)
notebook **noto** (*no-toe*)
note paper **memo yoshi** (*may-moe yoe-she*)
nylon **nairon** (*nie-rone*)

ointment, salve **nanko** (*nah-koe*)
out of stock **shina-gire** (*she-nah-gee-ray*)
overcoat **oba** (*oh-bahh*)

pajamas **pajama** (*pahjah-mah*)

pan **nabe** (*nah-bay*)

panties **panti** (*pahn-tee*)

paste **nori** (*no-ree*)

pencil **enpitsu** (*en-peet-sue*)

pendant **pendanto** (*pen-dahn-toe*)

perfume **kosui** (*koe-sue-ee*)

personal computer **paso-kon** (*pah-so-kone*)

pillow **makura** (*mah-kuu-rah*)

playing card **toranpu** (*toe-rahn-puu*)

pliers **penchi** (*pen-chee*)

plug (*electrical*) **puragu** (*puu-rah-guu*);
   also **sashi-komi** (*sah-she-koe-me*)

pocket **poketto** (*poe-ket-toe*)

polyester **poriesuteru** (*poe-ree-ss-tay-rue*)

postcard **hagaki** (*hah-gah-kee*)

print (*photograph*) **purinto** (*puu-reen-toe*)

pullover **puruoba** (*puu-rue-oh-bah*)

radio **rajio** (*rah-jee-oh*)

radio-cassette player **raji-kase** (*rahjee-kah-say*)

raincoat **rein-koto** (*rain-koe-toe*)

rayon **reyon** (*ray-yone*)

razor **kami-sori** (*kah-me-soe-ree*)

razor blade **kami-sori no ha** (*kah-me-soe-ree no hah*)

receipt **ryoshu-sho** (*rio-shuu-show*)

record **rekodo** (*ray-koe-doe*)

ribbon **ribon** (*ree-bone*)

road map **doro chizu** (*doe-roe chee-zuu*);
   also **rodo-mappu** (*roe-doe-mah-puu*)

safety pin **anzen pin** (*ahn-zen-peen*)

sale **seru** (*say-rue*)

sandal **sandaru** (*sahn-dah-rue*)

sanitary napkin
   seiri-yo napukin (*say-ree-yoe nahp-keen*)

satin **saten** (*sah-ten*)

saw (cutting) **nokogiri** (*no-koe-ghee-ree*)

scarf **sukafu** (*sue-kahh-fuu*)

screwdriver **doraiba** (*doe-rye-bah*)

shampoo **shanpu** (*shahn-puu*)

shaving cream
　shebingu kurimu (*shay-bean-guu kuu-ree-muu*)

sheet **shitsu** (*sheet-sue*)

shirt **waishatsu** (*wie-shaht-sue*)

shoe **kutsu** (*koot-sue*)

shoe polish **kutsu -zumi** (*koot-sue-zuu-me*)

shoestring **kutsuhimo** (*koot-sue-he-moe*)

shorts (underwear) **burifu** (*buu-ree-fuu*);
　pantsu (*pant-sue*)

silk **kinu** (*kee-nuu*)

skirt **sukato** (*sue-kahh-toe*)

slacks **surakkusu** (*sue-rock-sue*)

sleeve **sode** (*soe-day*)

　long sleeve **naga-sode** (*nah-gah-soe-day*)
　　short sleeve **han-sode** (*han-soe-day*)

slip **surippu** (*sue-reep-puu*)

slipper **surippa** (*sue-reep-pah*)

sneaker **sunikka** (*sue-neek-kah*)

soap **kesho sekken** (*kay-show sake-ken*)

sock **kutsu-shita** (*koot-sue-ssh-tah*)

sock (athletic) **sokkusu** (*soe-kuu-suu*)

sold out **uri-kire** (*uu-ree-kee-ray*)

speaker (stereo) **supika** (*spee-kah*)

special price **tokka** (*toke-kah*)

sponge **suponji** (*sue-pone-jee*)

stamp **kitte** (*key-tay*)

stapler **hochikisu** (*hoe-chee-key-sue*)

stationery **binsen** (*bean-sen*)

stocking **sutokkingu** (*sue-toke-keen-guu*)

string **himo** (*he-moe*)

suede **suedo** (*sway-doe*)

suit (men's) **sebiro** (*say-bee-roe*); also **sutsu** (*sue-t'sue*)

suntan lotion **santan roshon** (*sahn-tahn roe-shoan*)

super special price **cho tokka** (*choe toke-kah*)

sweater **seta** (*say-tah*)

tape (cellophane) **sero-tepu** (*say-roe-tay-puu*)

tape recorder **tepu rekoda** (*tay-puu-ray-koe-dah*)

television set **terebi-setto** (*tay-ray-bee-set-toe*)

thermometer (body) **taion-kei** (*tie-own-kay-e*)

thermometer (room) **ondo-kei** (*ohn-doe-kay-e*)

thermos jug **maho-bin** (*mah-hoe-bean*)

tissue paper (Kleenex) **tisshu-pepa** (*tish-yuu-pay-pah*)

toaster **tosta** (*toas-tah*)

toilet paper **toiretto-pepa** (*toe-e-rate-toe-pay-pah*)

toothbrush **ha-burashi** (*hah-buu-rah-she*)

toothpaste **ha-migaki** (*hah-me-gah-kee*)

topcoat **koto** (*koe-toe*)

toy **omocha** (*oh-moe-chah*)

trash **gomi** (*go-me*)

trash basket **kuzu-kago** (*kuu-zuu-kah-go*);
   also **kuzu-ire** (*kuu-zuu-ee-ray*)

tray **o-bon** (*oh-bone*)

trousers **zubon** (*zuu-bone*)

T-shirt **ti-shatsu** (*tee-shaht-sue*)

underwear **shita-gi** (*ssh-tah-ghee*)

velvet **birodo** (*bee-roe-doe*)

video recorder **bideo-rekoda** (*bee-day-oh-ray-koe-dah*)

vitamin **bitamin** (*bee-tah-meen*)

vitamin pill **bitamin-zai** (*bee-tah-meen-zie*)

watch **tokei** (*toe-kay-e*)

wool **uru** (*uu-rue*)

wristwatch **ude-dokei** (*uu-day-doe-kay-e*)

APPENDIX

Shopping and
Transportation Maps

Ginza-Yanagi-dōri 銀座柳通り

Ginza - Itchōme 銀座 1丁目

ki-Za ▲

Ⓢ Mikimoto

Meidiya Ⓢ

Ⓢ Ginza Melsa

🏛 Tōkyō Central Art Museum

inza

Ⓢ Signas ▲

Chanel

Cartier

Ⓢ Tiffany & Co
Ⓢ Itoya

MS

Ⓢ Louis Vuitton

Ⓢ Matsuya

ASEAN Center

Chūō-dōri 中央通り

Azuma-dōri あづま通り

銀座三原通り

Mihara-dōri 三原通り

Ⓢ Nelson's Bar

▲ Yomiko

Seiyō Ginza Ⓗ

Ginza Saison Theater

▲ Ginza Yu

▲ Arimura Line

Tokuracho 徳町

KYOBASHI PARK

★

sukoshi

mi-dōri

Shōwa-dōri 昭和通り

銀座通り

Higashi Ginza 東銀座

Ⓗ Ginza Daiei

▲ Magazine House

🐾 Kabuki-za Theater

⊠

KAMEIBASHI PARK

★

Ginza Tōkyō Hotel Atamiso Ⓗ

Higashi Ginza 東銀座

Hibiya Line 営田日比谷線

Ⓗ Ginza Tōkyū

▲ Nissan

⊠

Ⓗ Ginza Marunouchi

TSUKIJI (1) 築地 1丁目

TSUKIJI (3) 築地 3丁目

Tsukiji 築地

⬆ N

Ginza
(Tokyo)

卍 Tsukiji Hongan-Ji

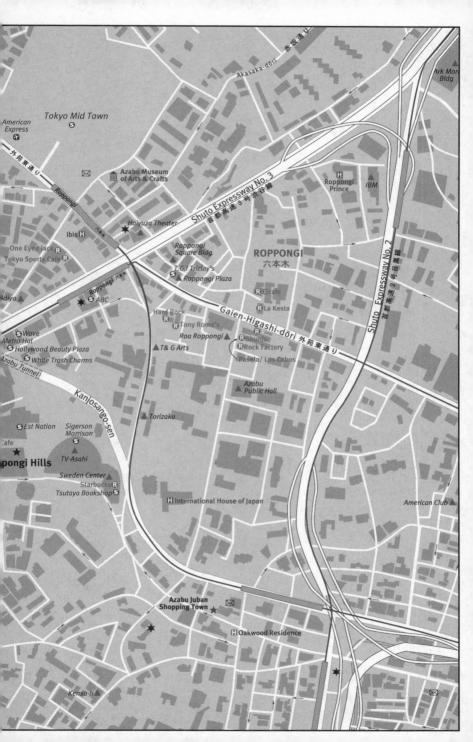

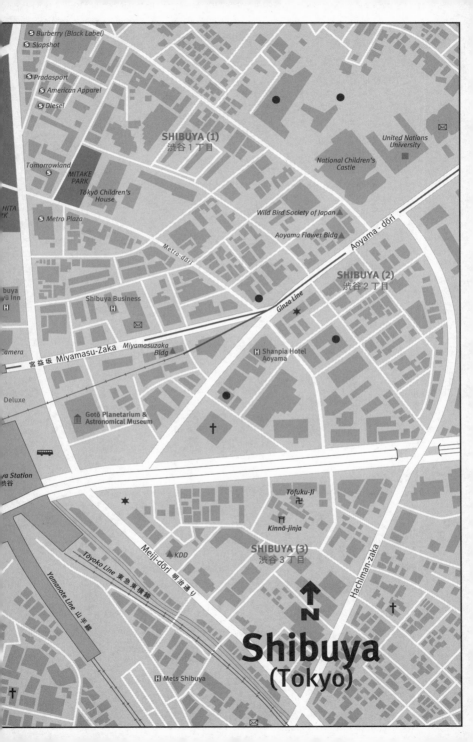

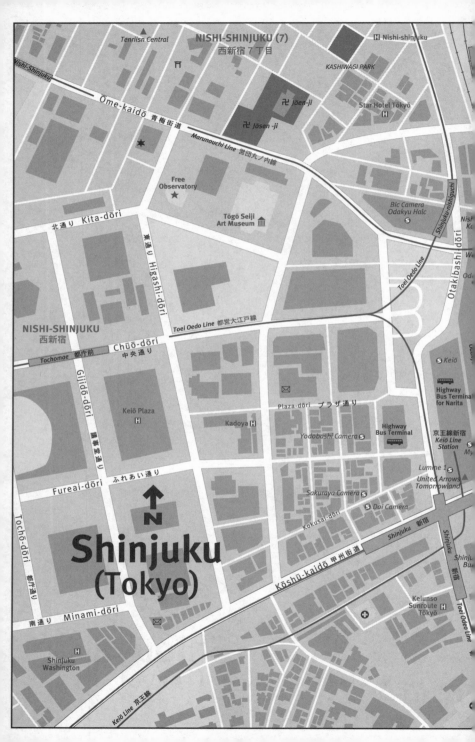

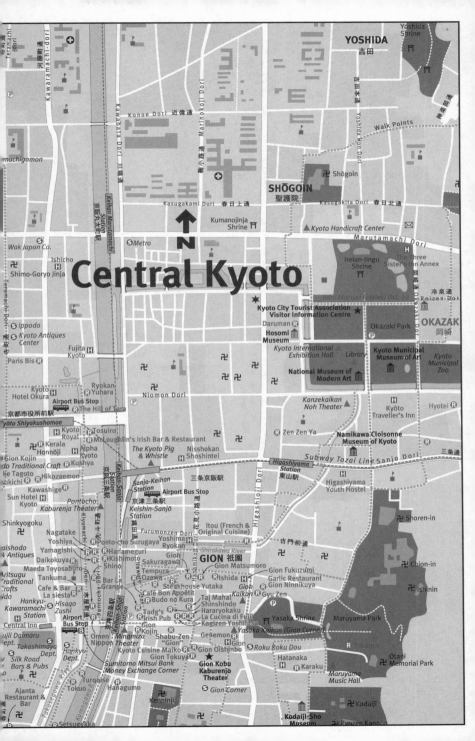

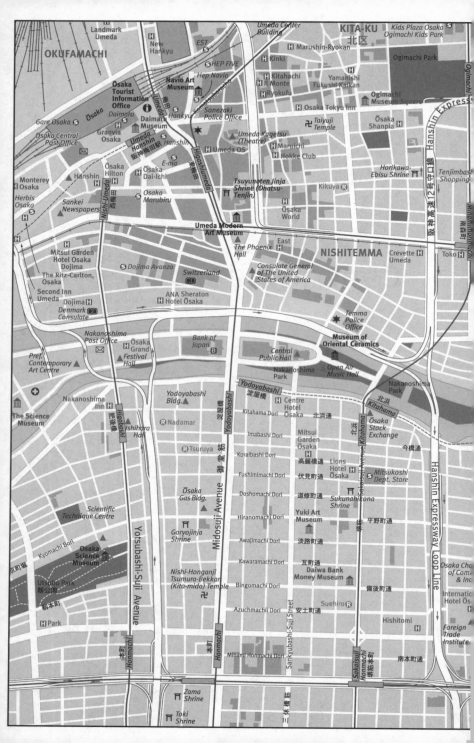

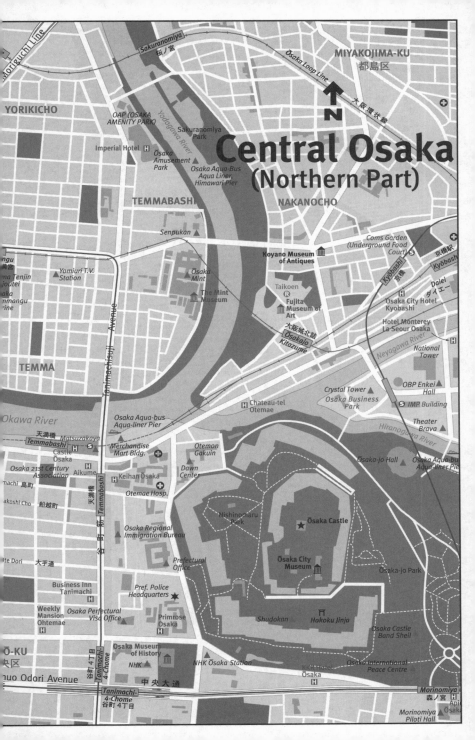

Ecchu Park

† St. Maria Cathedral

▲ Otsuki Nohgaku-do Hall

Tamatsukuri-inari Shrine

見緑地線
Tsurumi Ryokuchi Line
nachi

Tanimachi-6-Chome
谷町6丁目

長堀通

Nagahori-Dori Avenue

玉造
Tamatsukuri

Uehommachisuji-Dori Avenue

上本町筋通

卍 Shrine

Enjuan Temple
卍

Sanadayama Park

卍 Kozujinja Shrine

谷町9丁目
Tanimachi-9-Chome

前通

Izuma Hosp.

鶴橋
Tsuruhashi

Uehommachi Hi-Hi Town ▲

上本町
Uehommachi
Ⓢ Kintetsu

Ⓗ Miyako Hotel Ōsaka

鶴橋駅
Tsuruhashi

Korean Market Ⓢ

Ⓗ The Live-Artex

✚

✚ ✚

Ⓗ International House (Belgium Flanders Museum)

Environment Science Laboratory
Environment Polution Surveillance Centre

卍 Kisshoji

Ⓗ Yoshino Ryokan

TENNŌJI-KU
天王寺区

Momodani Park

卍

図

四天王寺前

Ⓗ Takaraya
✚

Shitennoji-Mae

Momodani
桃谷

★

✚

N

卍
Shitennoji

✚

Central Osaka
(Southern Part)

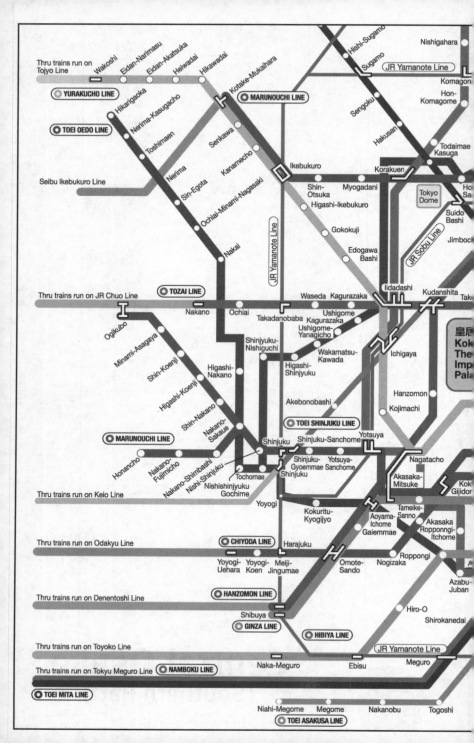

SUBWAYS IN TOKYO